CHINESE GODS

D0615877

CHINESE GODS

Jonathan Chamberlain

Pelanduk
Publications

Published by
Pelanduk Publications (M) Sdn. Bhd.,
24 Jalan 20/16A, 46300 Petaling Jaya,
Selangor Darul Ehsan, Malaysia.

All correspondence to:
Pelanduk Publications (M) Sdn. Bhd.,
P.O. Box 8265, 46785 Kelana Jaya,
Selangor Darul Ehsan, Malaysia.

All rights reserved.
Copyright © 1987 Jonathan Chamberlain.
All rights reserved. No part of this book may be reproduced in any
form or by any means without prior permission from the Publisher.
Front Cover: God of War (Guangong) is flanked by his two attendants –
Zhoucang on his right and Guanping on his left.

ISBN 967-978-105-4

1st printing 1987
2nd printing 1988
3rd printing 1989
4th printing 1995

Printed by
Eagle Trading Sdn. Bhd.

Dedication

*I dedicate this book to my immediate ancestors,
Terence and Joan Chamberlain.*

Foreword

Judging from ancient records dating back many thousands of years, there have always been two Chinese concepts of the Ultimate, one scholarly and impersonal, the other popular and theistic. The first is represented by the Chinese character for Heaven, *Tien;* the second by two names, one meaning Heavenly Lord, the other meaning High Emperor. (Much later, these two theistic terms were adopted by the Catholic and Protestant missionaries respectively to represent their concept of an Almighty Creator God.) By the time of Confucius about 2,500 years ago, it would seem that, among educated Chinese people, the impersonal concept of the Ultimate had become widely accepted, leaving the theistic one to the masses, who developed around it what might be called China's folk-religion. Confucius, and his followers through the ages, have regarded the Ultimate as an impersonal source of existence or dynamic happening rather than a being. Thinking and acting in accordance with the workings of that source would, so they believed, bring harmony and happiness as a reward. Acting out of accord with it, or acting against it, would bring disaster. Confucius did not absolutely disbelieve in the existence of gods and spirits (subordinate to the Ultimate); he advised his followers to treat them with respect but keep at a distance from them. He and others who held the same view might well be called high-principled agnostics; who, though prepared to believe in the reality of supernatural beings, felt that having relations with them would be unwise for human beings and not in accordance with the Heavenly Order or rules to which we would be well advised to adhere.

However, until not very long ago in China (as in most other countries until this century), about 80 per cent of the people were illiterate. Of the remaining 20 per cent, perhaps half were no more than semi-literate. It would seem that, throughout the ages, the more highly literate Chinese were to various degrees agnostic and tended, if not to doubt the existance of supernatural beings, then at least to question their power to be of any use to us. It is true that all officials, from the Emperor downwards, were at times required to offer petitions and make reports to Heaven, as though a supreme God or a hierarchy of supernatural beings actually governed our lives. However, such ceremonies seem to have been for the purpose of satisfying the common people that their welfare was being properly looked after at all levels by the officials; it does not, I think, denote positive belief in the existance of the celestial beings they formally addressed amidst the smoke of burnt offerings.

On the other hand, the great masses of the people were, as I have said, illiterate. These common people, constituting an overwhelming majority, seem to have been fully convinced of the existence of supernatural beings, of whom a vast hierarchy came to be recognized within the compass of the folk-religion. Many of those beings are mentioned in very early Chinese texts; other were admitted to the hierarchy from time to time; still others were in fact human beings posthumously deified either by the reigning emperor or by popular acclaim. One could say that the Chinese masses were exceedingly credulous and willing to believe in all sorts and kinds of marvels; whereas they were ruled by learned scholars varying from agnostics to convinced "atheists" Note, however, that, as the Chinese literati never recognized a clear distinction between spirit and matter, the term atheist does not really apply. Mystical belief in spirit and matter as one indivisible whole (the *Tao*) was widespread; thus the scholars were by no means materialists, being sceptical only as to the existence of spirit or spirits as apart from matter, or matter as apart from spirit.

By the beginning of the Christian Era, a separate religion, namely Taoism, had been developed. Some of its founders had originally been itinerant medicos searching for cures for illness and means to prolong youth, vigour and life itself; others had been devotees of the profound philosophy of Lao-tze and Chuang-tze. Taoists thenceforth tended to be wanderers or else to form small communities in isolated places in the mountains, practising their philosophy and skills effectively, so that they remained vigorous to a great age and lived long. Buddhism arrived in China officially in the first century of the Christian Era, but probably a good deal before that time. The earliest Buddhist patriarchs were Indians or else Chinese who had adopted Indians as their teachers. They liked to build their temples both in the great cities and also in isolated mountainous retreats. Thenceforward, varying numbers of people could specifically be called Taoists or Buddhists and regarded as being largely separate religiously both from the masses and from the body of learned scholars. During most periods, Confucianism remained the only religion or philosophy acceptable in public life among the ruling classes, even at those times when the Imperial Household itself leaned strongly towards Buddhism, Taoism or both. The majority of ordinary people, however, continued to believe in an ever-increasing number of heavenly beings, so the folk-religion prospered among them in almost all reigns. As we have seen, some of the deities date from remote antiquity, while others were added to the pantheon as the centuries passed by. These supernatural beings include stellar deities, nature deities, deified humans and many, many other sorts. The common people incorporated in this vast pantheon all the gods, spirits and Bodhisattvas they heard about during intercourse with Taoists and Buddhists, making a total of over a million. So it can be said that they amalgamated elements of four religions and/or philosophies of life; namely, Confucianism, Taoism, Buddhism and the folk-religion (which, however, has never borne that or any other designation in Chinese, remaining nameless throughout the ages).

The Chinese, themselves, have always spoken of their having but three religions. The folk-religion is my own term for the fourth (and, in some ways, earliest of all). The reason for the omission is as follows. Until not much more than a hundred years ago, there was no particular word in the Chinese language precisely meaning "religion". The absence of such a word seems to have been due to the Chinese unwillingness to except any discrimination between spirit and matter, thus leaving no scope for a separation of religion and life. In the 19th century, however, a word for "religion" became necessary for the purpose of translating foreign texts into Chinese, so the term *tsung-chiao* (*dzoong-jiao*) was borrowed from Japan. By that time, however, the Chinese had long been used to talking of *san-chiao* (*san-jiao*) meaning "The Three Teachings". In short, the word for "teaching" had hitherto been used in place of "religion". The folk-religion could not properly be called a "teaching", because no philosophical or moral teaching of any kind was included in it. Most people prayed for boons to the gods of their choice and made offerings in the hope of appeasing divine anger and thus keeping out of all kinds of trouble. The folk-religion included very little else than prayers and offerings together with certain rituals that evolved round these two practices. As a result of constantly hearing the term "three religions". (never four), the Chinese themselves became confused. To this day, it is common to hear even knowledgeable Chinese designating a temple that is not obviously Confucian or Buddhist by the adjective "Taoist". Thus Taoism and the folk-reli-religion have become confused in people's minds. This situation is also due to the fact that Taoist communities living in solitary mountain places needed some form of support. This they obtained locally, largely in the form of eatables and other necessities donated by surrounding peasants. In return for such gifts, they had to provide what the peasants most wanted, namely: first and foremost, medicine; second, obsequies for the dead; third, picturesque ceremonies in honour of certain gods, particularly on the supposed birthdays of those deities. Thus it came about that Taoist hermits, who might personally have no particular religious beliefs, found themselves involved in curing the sick and in carrying out colourful religious ceremonies to satisfy their clients.

I do not quite agree with a statement made by the author of this book that, properly speaking, the Chinese have had only one religion. Outside the folk-religion, there have long been many Chinese who could properly be called Confucians; others who could properly be called Taoists or Buddhists or Muslims. However, it is true that the great mass of common people subscribed to an amalgam of the four. To that extent, the author's statement is correct.

In this book, the author has picked out some representative deities belonging to the folk-religion and described them, giving a colourful picture of aspects of Chinese traditional belief as it was among the masses. The prevalence of folk-religion temples to this day in Taiwan, Hong Kong, most big cities of Southeast Asia and other places with large Chinese communities indicates that the folk-religion is very much alive. Its temples are often thronged from early morning till late at night. Surprisingly, many of these modern worshippers appear to be well-to-do and therefore, presumably well-educated. On the Chinese mainland, since the devastation of temples that took place during the Cultural Revolution, one does not see many such temples, for they are more strikingly redolent of mere superstition than those belonging to the other religions, and therefore especially abhorent to communists; but it is extremely likely that the folk-religion is still very much alive in a quiet way. Not being institutionized in the same way as others, it can secretly survive in a hostile environment, ready to bloom again when hostility abates.

I think one reason why well-off and apparently well-educated people in Chinese overseas' communities adhere in large numbers to the folk-religion is that most of these now prosperous people are the children or grandchildren of illiterate immigrants from whom they have inherited peasant superstitions and little else in the cry of tradition.

Surprisingly little has hitherto been written about the deites of the folk-religion. The fact that is still lingers on and, indeed, has blossomed among those overseas communities despite their degree of sophistication, suggests that it is highly for English-language readers interested in things Chinese to learn something of the ancient beliefs which, over the centuries, led to the development of this very colourful religion. I am therefore delighted to write this foreword to Jonathan Chamberlain's book. May it become the forerunner of longer and more detailed books on analogous themes. Our author writes well. That he covers only a few of the innumerable deities is entirely excusable, in that this is a pioneer work. I personally hope he will be among the writers who, as times goes on, will give us a wider and deeper understanding of the Gods of China.

John Blofeld
The Mating Dragon Pavilion,
House of Wind and Clouds,
Year of the Hare.

Also of interest:-
Spectrum of Chinese Culture
Lee Siow Mong

To the many millions of overseas Chinese, whose forefathers came and settled in an adopted land, Chinese culture or tradition remains merely a "practice", a mode of life or behaviour. They have little or no understanding of what these traditions mean or how they came about.

In this book Tan Sri Lee Siow Mong has recorded for the benefit of present and future generations, a wide spectrum of traditional Chinese cultural practices and beliefs, emphasizing throughout, how and why they developed. This is truly a record of the author's knowledge of a lifetime. He has lived and grown up under the shadow of Chinese Culture.

China, he says, developed an unbroken culture for thousand of years and, although many elements of Chinese culture today were not found in ancient times, and many elements of ancient times are not found today, Chinese culture is the better and richer for it. A culture will be poor and backward if it is rigid and unwilling to absorb the good and practical from other cultures, notes the author. Chinese culture is rich and enduring precisely because of its practical wisdom and absorbing power.

This book should prove to be of great interest to Chinese searching for ways to maintain their cultural roots within a modern context. For others who want to know and understand Chinese culture, the author takes them through from the days of antiquity, when Chinese culture was moulded, to present-day practices and beliefs.

Contents

Acknowledgements

I am by no means a Chinese scholar and so I have been extremely fortunate in having at hand friends who have given me a great deal of valuable help. Above all I would like to thank my wife Bernadette Sau-fong without whose constant help I can honestly say this book would not have been possible; Laurent Sagart and John Thompson for their help with references and translations, and for listening critically to some of the hypotheses put forward in this book, Ann Broomfield for providing information on the history of glass painting, Stephen Peplow for his criticism which forced me to re-organize Part I of this book, and Philip Rosenberg for his enthusiasm and help, without which this book might not have seen print. There were many others whose help in small things contributed immensely to this book. Most of them were strangers. To them all I am indebted. Inevitably there will be errors in the following pages and, for these, I alone am responsible.

This book is not an academic work and for that reason I have not felt bound to identify exact origins of quotes or of particular pieces of information. Nor do I now intend to give an exhaustive bibliography. However there are books to which I am indebted. My standard reference books were V.R. Burkhardt's *Chinese Creeds and Customs* (the original three volume edition), Williams's *Outlines of Chinese Symbolism and Art Motives* (which has the immense value of being simple and factual) and Feuchtwang's *An Anthropological Analysis of Chinese Geomancy*. This last book was published by a now defunct Laotian publishing house and is no longer in print. I have borrowed unashamedly from it especially in those sections dealing with the magic square.

When it was necessary to confirm the Chinese name of a mythological character I would repair to Swindons bookshop in Kowloon and consult E.T.C. Werner's *Dictionary of Chinese Mythology* — the price of this volume ensured that it would not leave the shelves. On the development of Chinese civilization and religion, Marcel Granet's classics *Chinese Civilization* and *The Religion of the Chinese People* cannot be bettered. On the development of the various strands of what is normally clumped under the term Taoism there is only one book worth considering — Holmes Welch's *Taoism: The Parting of the Way*. Despite at least one error of fact (he states that the "Pan" in Kunshu P'an and Lu Pan are the same), Dennis Bloodworth's *The Chinese Machiavelli* gives a highly readable account of Chinese history. *Early Ming Government* by Edward Farmer gives the fullest account available in English of the Emperor Yung-lo. Without this book I could not have reached the conclusions I did in the chapter on Na Cha. Finally Gertrude and James Jobes' *Outer Space: Myths, Name Meanings, Calendars* provided an invaluable summary of the cosmological systems of all the ancient civilizations and I have relied on this book for all information relating to the stars.

Jonathan Chamberlain

Table of Dynasties

HSIA	1990 – 1557 BC
SHANG	1557 – 1027 BC
CHOU	1027 – 221 BC
Spring and Autumn Period	722 – 481 BC
The Warring States	481 – 221 BC
CH'IN	221 – 207 BC
HAN	202 BC – 220 AD
THREE KINGDOMS	220 – 265 AD
PERIOD OF DISUNION	280 – 589 AD
SUI	589 – 618 AD
T'ANG	618 – 906 AD
FIVE DYNASTIES	906 – 960 AD
SUNG	960 – 1127 AD
NORTHERN KIN & SOUTHERN SUNG (PARTITION)	1127 – 1279 AD
YUAN (Mongol)	1260 – 1368 AD
MING	1368 – 1644 AD
CH'ING (Manchu)	1644 – 1912 AD

Introduction

This world is full of instant experts. It is easy to appear knowledgeable about a subject such as Chinese religion when so little has been written on the subject. There are those who will confidently assert that the Chinese have three religions and even go so far as to name them. I am not one of these. I believe that the Chinese have one religion, one that is nameless, untheologized and abiding. This book is my attempt to unravel some of the threads of that religion. The reader should read this book as he would a travelogue. It is an adventure in uncharted territory where only a few other travellers have gone before.

My journey started when I saw a number of curious, and rather brash, paintings hanging at the back of a general store. I bought six and hung them in my sitting room. They were images of Gods painted on glass. They looked lonely so I acquired a few more and when I thought I had an entire set I discovered another. As my collection grew so did my interest in the Gods depicted. I set out to remedy my ignorance. Easier said than done. I had imagined that the bookshop would produce a volume capable of rectifying the fault. It didn't. The public library was no better. My curiosity did not abate and I managed to gain access to the university library. I headed for the files on Chinese Religion. More than a hundred books were listed. There were books on Taoism, Confucianism, Buddhism, Islam and Christianity and on the various combinations but there was not one book that even mentioned Chinese Gods.

Can Gods exist without a religion?

I eventually discovered that the few books of value were to be found under *Chinese Cults* and *Chinese Mythology* . My Chambers Dictionary gives the following definitions:

Cult: A system of religious belief: formal worship, a sect; an unorthodox or false religion; a great, often excessive admiration for a person or idea.

Myth: An ancient, traditional story of gods or heroes, especially one offering an explanation of some fact or phenomenon; figment; a commonly-held belief that is untrue or without foundation.

We see that neither of these words is very complimentary. Cult may mean "a system of religious belief" but we would not refer to Christianity as a cult. Implicit in the idea of religion is the concept of revealed truth while the word "cult" breathes mass deception.

What has happened? I think that this is clear. People who are interested in "religion" are interested in "universal truth".

They go in search of written expressions of this truth. They study them and discourse upon them. Christianity (to them) is not the worship of God in church on Sunday but the theological backing that great theological minds have developed over the centuries. It is theology that determines religion. Those who went to China to study Taoism, for example, devoted most of their energies to studying the book *Tao Te Ching* attributed to Lao Tzu. The fact that Lao Tzu was worshipped in temples and that "Taoist" priests officiated at ceremonies was seen as deviant and "cultic" and therefore worth little of their precious time.

On the question of mythology. The more I read the more dissatisfied I became. Those who collected myths simply presented them. They thought their presentation "scientific" because they had placed the stories into certain categories: Myths of fire, myths of epidemics etc. The result is unedifying. One damn God follows another. Incidents precede and succeed each other haphazardly. But where do they all fit in? Do they fit in? Mythology, clearly, is a category where gobbets of exotic beliefs can be deposited and quietly forgotten.

Having reached this position very early on, my interest was aroused. I still thought it would be relatively simple to piece together the information I found in various sources, put it together and provide a handbook for the occasional temple visitor. It has not turned out that way. At some point along the way I pierced a veil, something new and strange was revealed. I have been led on a trail that wound through the history, language and symbolic system of the Chinese. It has been a fascinating journey but not without dangers. It is worth looking at some of these dangers.

The Chinese language and the translation of this into English was the first major barrier I had to confront. The romanization of Chinese sounds divorces the sound from the character and thus from its meaning. The following example provides a good illustration of this.

I was researching the Miao Shan legends connected with Kuan Yin and discovered that, according to one authority, these can be traced to a monk named "Tao Suan". No characters were given. As *Tao* can mean "the way" I immediately assumed that the name meant "follower of the way," or some such thing, and I thought it strange that a Buddhist monk should have such an obviously Taoist name. Looking it up in my pocket phonetic dictionary I found that the combination of *Tao* and *Suan* could produce:

Garrulous Lion

To calculate plunder

Garlic curtain

Sour Herring

Painful sword

This is disregarding other romanizations *T'ao* and *Hsuan.* Again, was this monk anything to do with the Monk Xuan mentioned in connection with the God Na Cha?

For myself, I have not followed any specific system of romanization. I have generally followed in the steps of others. Sometimes I have used the Mandarin romanization, sometimes the Cantonese — whichever seemed most practical.

Chinese script offers another problem. Most characters are composed of two or more elements, each of which has its own individual meaning. To what extent does the final composite character depend on these subsidiary meanings? To take an example, *fang*, (坊) , (earth + square) meaning district, clearly depends on its elements. We can say that *fang* is a proper ideograph. Standard academic opinion on the subject is that only ten per cent of Chinese characters can be seen as ideographs. I find this very difficult to square with a very ancient and compelling insistence that words must accord with the things they refer to. If they don't, the system becomes unbalanced and disaster results. This belief is one of the cornerstones of Confucian belief. I have therefore taken the view that much can be learnt by breaking characters down into their elements.

At the level of speech we are faced with different problems. Mandarin has only 420 monosyllables and four tones making 1680 distinct sound units into which all the meanings it is possible to express must be fitted. In fact only a little over 1200 sound units are used. The Chinese like a good pun and their language allows a wealth of possibility. Similarities of sound also suggest to the Chinese associations of meaning. The bat is a common symbol of happiness because both words are pronounced *Fu*.

This book is about Chinese Gods and the meanings they embody. I have chosen to illustrate the book with photographs of glass paintings of the Gods. These images are not simply representations of the Gods. They are residences of the Gods. While I was in Singapore I read the report of a divorce case which concerned precisely this distinction.

A factory worker and his wife had had a fight in the course of which she had picked up the "House God" and broken it. It was clearly a deliberate act and capable of only one interpretation. The worker now wished to obtain a divorce not on the grounds that the marriage had irrepairably broken down but on the grounds that his wife had broken the God of the household. The magistrate decided there was a moot legal distinction involved and attempted to convince the man that his wife had not really broken the God itself, only its image. The worker refused to accept this. She had broken the God. The argument went on for over an hour before the worker conceded the point. Whether or not he really was convinced is debatable. With education, articulacy and situation against him it is impressive that he held out for so long – after all, what he really wanted was a divorce, which, happily, he obtained.

The idea of painting on glass appears to have originated in Byzantium some eight hundred years ago and by the fourteenth century, glass paintings were being produced in Italy. Leonardo da Vinci suggested that paintings be made directly on glass and seen through it so that there would be no diffusion of light from the surface of the paint. This advice was ignored by the great artists of the West but taken up by peasant craftsmen who found glass to be cheaper than wood. Mostly they painted the images of saints. Glass ikons of this type were being produced in parts of Czechoslovakia up to the beginning of this century.

While the Chinese have had glass for nearly two thousand years, they do not appear to have painted on it until after contact was established with the Dutch in the seventeenth century. One expert I talked to placed the origin of Chinese glass painting at the beginning of the Ch'ing dynasty (1644) but the earliest he had seen was from the late 1700's. Interestingly, the Chinese have restricted their use of glass to portraiture – such paintings are of people or of Gods.

Glass paintings of the type that illustrate this book can be found in most market areas. They are strikingly uniform, suggesting that they are in some way mass-produced on some sort of machine. One shop owner I talked to claimed that there was, in fact, a machine that pressed the image to the glass and when I expressed interest he gave me the address of his supplier.

The workshop was on the first floor of a narrow street in Shamshuipo. As I made my way to it I imagined – tried to imagine – the type of machinery used. Is it like a steam press of the kind used in laundries? Would it resemble a printing press?

If such a machine exists I am no closer to an answer. The man who opened the door grudgingly allowed me to enter and ignored me while I inspected his cramped space. No production was taking place and there were no machines. I did however see glass paintings in various stages of completion. Clearly an assembly line system of manufacture was used, but equally clearly this man's pictures were being produced by hand. The stages of production I saw were:

1. An outline of the entire picture, in some detail, was drawn in silver paint on the glass. It may have been traced by placing the glass over a paper image and copying the lines.
2. The hair was painted on and then the clothes.
3. The face was painted on last and the characters added.
4. The red backing was then rolled on.

Between each stage the paint had to be allowed to dry.

This process explains the extent of the similarity, as well as the stylistic unity, to be found.

The fact that these glass paintings are still being produced in reasonably large numbers is evidence that the Gods are still important and have not been displaced by more modern theologies. These Gods do not exist in a vacuum. In Part One of this book I have attempted to give some idea of the symbolic constellation to which they belong.

In Part Two I have tried to piece together, like a jigsaw, the identities of nineteen Gods. These Gods are the major Gods of the Chinese pantheon with one or two that are of purely local interest.

Part One:
The System

Fung-sui, Temples, Cities and Squares

To understand Chinese thought fully one must understand his symbolic systems. Few Chinese understand the system in its entirety though they make use of it. Because symbolism is important there are experts in the field whose job is to manipulate these symbols to create a favourable ambience in particular situations. By manipulating symbols this expert is in fact manipulating natural and supernatural forces to bring about certain desired effects. When a man wants to build a house, or arrange the furniture in an office or find a suitable site for a grave he will call in an expert in *Fung-sui*.

Fung-sui is the science of manipulating or judging the environment. *Fung-sui* literally means "wind — water". I call it a science because the expert works with a compass and makes calculations on the basis of certain assumptions. It integrates and makes use of the entire gamut of symbolism that has grown up over the centuries.

Unfortunately, it is a science (or art if you prefer) about which little has been written. Its importance has been seriously under-rated by scholars both in China and in the West, for not only are houses sited according to geomantic considerations but towns and cities are as well. Canton is placed on the south side of a mountain and the north side of the river for geomantic but not practical reasons. Kuei Lin, considered to have one of the most remarkable landscapes in the world in which hills rise abruptly from the river plain in all directions, is not only sited well in the environment but alterations have been made to the environment to further enhance its position. Caves have been dug through the hills. The most important is the Cave of the Seven Stars to the east of the town. Presumably these caves allow beneficial influences to penetrate through the hills and mountains. They were not made for aesthetic reasons but for geomantic considerations.

One of the most basic concepts of *fung-sui* is the symbolism that attaches to the points of the compass. South refers to summer and life; north — winter and death; east — spring and harmony; west — autumn and harmony. The front door of a house or temple is always assumed to be facing south no matter what the true direction is. The forces of *Yin* and *Yang* also appear in the equation. Summer is the seat of *Yang*, the male principle, while north is the seat of *Yin*, the female. At the spring and autumn equinoxes, the two forces are in balance. In Chinese diagrams, south is placed in our north position because south is "up". *Fung-sui* compasses point south.

Chinese temples follow two basic models. The first is the *kung* — or palace, the second is the *miu* (Mandarin: *miao*). The typical *kung* is a large open court with a covered altar in the centre. Along the "north" wall there will be a further three altars. The *miu*, on the other hand, is almost an inverse image of this arrangement. Instead of being opened it is closed except for a hole in the roof in the centre. The main altar is in the centre of the back wall. A diagram of a typical *kung* can be found on the first page of the next chapter. This can be compared with the diagram below of an idealized *miu*.

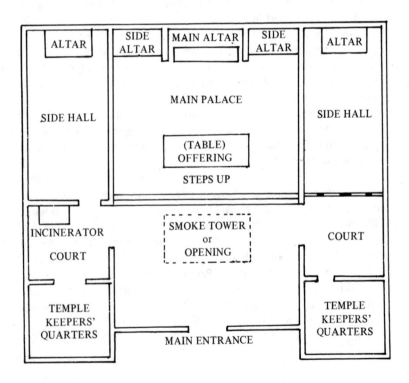

Map of Ch'ang An
During the T'ang Dynasty

1. Taming Palace
2. Hanyuan Hall
3. K'aiyuan
4. Imperial City
5. West Market

6. Yenp'ing
7. East Market
8. Leyu Park
9. Ch'ihsia Gate

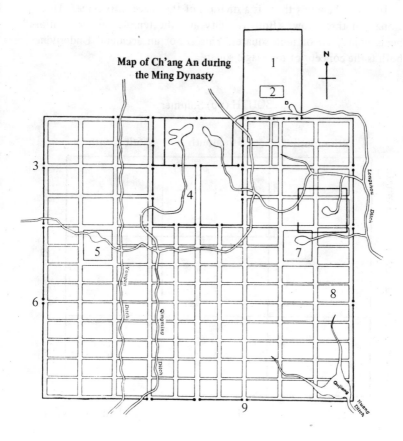

Map of Ch'ang An during
the Ming Dynasty

I have made an architectural distinction between the two types of temple but a small room boasting only one altar may be called a *kung* while a grand palace may be termed a *miu*. It depends largely on the honour appropriate to the God or Goddess enshrined in the structure. If we compare this diagram with the map of Ch'ang An, the Chinese capital during the T'ang dynasty we see that the Imperial City is situated in the place accorded the main altar in the *miu*. This is entirely appropriate as the character for *miu*, 廟 , is a roof of protection, 广 , over the character for dynasty, 朝 , which in turn is constructed from an alliance of the sun, 日 , and moon, 月 . The emperor was the "Son of Heaven" and he alone mediated between the universe and society.

In both diagrams there is a division of the space into threes. Three along and three down. Both the city and the temple can be seen as being composed of nine squares. This is not an accident. Underlying both is the concept of the magic square.

SOUTH (up) Summer

	4th month	5th month	6th month	
3rd month	4	9	2	7th month
2nd month	3	5	7	8th month
1st month	8	1	6	9th month
	12th month	11th month	10th month	

NORTH (down) Winter

The Lo Shu magic square was discovered by the Chinese over three thousand years ago. The even, or female numbers are placed in the corners while the odd, male numbers are at the cardinal points and at the centre. Add the numbers up in any line and they come to fifteen. In feudal times, the lord's mansion was divided into nine rooms and he rotated from one to the other throughout the year as he himself regulated the year on behalf of the people. The central square is the imperial square. There is a tension between the two positions — centre and north — as to which is most appropriate for the lord and emperor. North is the older position and brings the lord into closer association with the souls of the dead while the centre allies him more closely with the heavenly stars.

The magic square derives from an earlier construct — a square with a central fifth square.

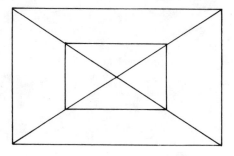

We find cities based on this model from India, through Egypt to Ireland, we find it also among the Aztecs. The four quarters are always related to four seasons. The city takes on a cosmological significance. Not only cities were so divided. Present day Ireland has four provinces but the celtic word for province is *coiced* which means a fifth. The fifth province was *meath* (Mide), the middle, the seat of the kings. The other four provinces correspond to the cardinal points of the compass and the seasons. China too was once divided into five provinces then became nine. In Ireland as in China the lord built a nine-roomed mansion which allows a division of the cosmology into twelve equal periods, Christ, the lord, had twelve disciples; the tribes of Israel were twelve in number; Odin was surrounded by twelve God councillors; the Athenians of Aristotle's time were divided into four tribes, each consisting of three phratries, each phratry comprised thirty families just as the month had thirty days.

China was not alone in basing their cosmological system on a square. In China the fields of the commune were divided into nines and the produce of the central square was given to the state. This is the well system as the well was in the central square — the Chinese character for well could not be more explicit (井).

The origin of the magic square is traditionally ascribed to the Emperior Yu, one of the mythical founding figures of China.

Hsing T'ien Temple

PLAN OF HSING T'IEN KUNG

4 Subordinates of Kuan Kung; his "Assessors"	Kuan Kung	Gate	Kuan Kung's 2 Parents + 2 Children
1. Wang Wun-tzu 2. Lu Tung-pin 3. Chang Wun-tzu 4. Yo Fei			

Kung Ming Chang Fei Lu Tung-pin	Hsing Tien	Confucius Buddha Lao Tzu

gate

Altar to the 3 Kwan

Side gate   main gate   Side gate

Every temple involves a juxtaposing of disparate elements of beliefs. These elements come from a wide variety of sources. Chinese beliefs have changed as the organizations of society changed. The major stages were pre-feudal, feudal and imperial (sometimes called bureaucratic feudal). The beliefs that were current at each stage left their residue in the stage that followed. Each temple manipulates these residues and places them within a framework that "makes sense".

This Hsing T'ien temple incorporates two major elements: the Gods of the pre-historical past who were founders of Chinese civilization and the Gods who were men and who were deified as a result of their actions on earth. The first is essentially feudal, the second imperial, Chinese religion is inseparable from its history. But one temple cannot incorporate residues from every stage in the development of the religion.

Chinese Folk Religion operates on too many different levels. First there are "animistic" beliefs evident in the worship of rocks, trees and springs. There are domestic, earth and harvest gods, star gods, mythical beings and deified persons. There is an imperial religion and a popular religion which were loosely bound together and drawn on each other. Just as the clan head worshipped at hills and streams 4,000 years ago, so in more recent times the emperor worshipped the sacred mountains and rivers of the empire. These early beliefs are overlaid with Buddhist and Taoist conceptions of Heaven and Hell. Throughout it all there is a unifying sense that admits of only one religion.

This temple lies a short train ride out of Taipei, Taiwan on the outskirts of Chung Yi. The scale is a surprise. The solid black figure of Hsing T'ien must be fifteen feet high, the court a hundred yards long. Entry is attained through the side gate; the main gate is closed, acting as a spirit screen. This is similar to most Catholic churches where the altar and crucifix rarely face out through an open door.

To the right of Hsing T'ien are statues of the three philosophers who have had most influence on Chinese thought. The Buddha's central position is not particularly significant. Outside there is a small shrine which gives Lao Tzu pride of place. Confucius, it seems, is never accorded this honour. It is not uncommon to find altars to these three and the only thing worth remarking on is that Confucius is given human form — usually he is represented by a plaque.

On Hsing T'ien's left are three figures with a militaristic flavour. Kung Ming and Chang Fei were historical figures who fought with Kuan Kung, who occupies the central altar at the back. Lu Tung-pin is one of the eight immortals. The importance of these eight immortals is grossly exaggerated. Supposedly the senior deans in the Taoist pantheon, they are said to have reached their position by understanding nature's secrets and thus attaining immortality. They are described as living on mushrooms and fungi on the Islands of the Blest somewhere beyond the horizon to the east of China. They are in fact purely symbolic caricatures of eight states of existence which have found favour among designers of pottery. The character for immortal, 仙 , is composed of the radical for man and the character for hill, 山 . The idea stems from the ancient idea of hills as sacred places, presided over by a spirit. In other contexts the character means fairy.

The idea of the eight immortals only came into existence during the Yuan dynasty (1260 – 1368). All eight are credited with magical powers and all are wanderers who refuse to be tied down by family or state. Lu Tung-pin is the warrior immortal whose emblem is the sword slung on his back and a fly whisk held in the right hand. "He traversed the earth, slaying dragons and ridding the world of various forms of evil for upwards of 400 years" (C.A.S. Williams).

Kuan Kung, the red-faced God of War, occupies the central altar at the back. He is the most powerful God in the Chinese pantheon. He owes his position to the fact that he embodies to the fullest extent all the virtues of a warrior and knight. He had a strong right arm and acted with utter rectitude at all times. With two blood brothers, Chang Fei and Liu Pei, he carved a place for himself in the history books during a time of great upheaval. On his right there is an altar to his family and on his left another in honour of his subordinates in his celestial ministry. Here we find again Lu Tung-pin and Chang Fei, under the guise of Chang Wan-tzu, Chang the saviour from danger. Wang Wun-tzu, the king who saves from danger can only be Liu Pei, the eldest of the three blood brothers. This threesome will be dealt with in a later chapter.

Yo Fei is another mighty warrior who gained a reputation for valour and loyalty. He reached his majority at a time when China had been over-run by tribal hordes from the north and west. The Chinese court had withdrawn south of the Yangtze river unfortunately leaving the emperor behind. Yo Fei organized an army and led them into battle against the Kin. The Kin cavalry had adopted the hitherto successful tactic of placing heavily armoured men on horses bound together in threes. When they charged the momentum was irresistible. Yo Fei prudently adopted a different tactic which involved getting out of the way and regrouping. He named it the Start Scatter and it proved most effective. His successes however proved rather embarrassing to the new emperor who feared that his brother might be rescued. He recalled Yo Fei and murdered him.

There now remains the small side altar to the three Kwan, or officers. They are mythical rulers of China known for their wisdom and for the harmony they established. Their names are Yao, Shun and Yu. This altar appears to disturb the symmetry of the temple; balance can only be re-established if we bring the open side-gate into the equation. Gates are dangerous. They allow the entry of evil.

If we had to choose one word that summed up Chinese ambitions in the religious sphere that word would be "harmony". Harmony however can only occur in a closed system. Change is a constant threat. Only a static system can provide the ingredients necessary for harmony and balance. Gates allow change in. It was in defence of harmony that both the Chinese and the Japanese shut their doors to the West for centuries.

Looking at the temple as a whole again we see that those figures who represent stability and harmony are ranged on the right, east, while the military defenders of the state are seated on the left, west, on which side too is the gate, symbolic of danger. At the centre is Hsing T'ien, God of the Moving Heavens also called Huang Ti, the Yellow Emperor, the founder of Chinese civilization.

From Myth to History

Chinese historians have always patterned their past according to philosophical precepts. If the facts are inconsistent with the image of the past, they are interpreted into submission. Chinese history posits an age of the Five Sovereigns, the first of which was Huang Ti. Prior to this age, tradition tells of an age of the 3 August Ones: Fu Hsi, Nu Kua and Shen-nung. The importance of the number five, long established, necessitated that there be five sovereigns. If this hadn't happened the founding figures would have been Yao and Shun, the earliest of all figures mentioned, who were subsequently relegated to the positions of fourth and fifth emperors of the age of the Five Sovereigns. This means that the attributes and creations of Fu Hsi are also those of Huang Ti and of Yao.

To Fu Hsi is attributed the teaching of how to fish, hunt and tend to flocks; to Huang Ti agriculture, language, culture, the forms of marriage, the division of lands and the organization of the calendar. These too are attributed to Yao. The identification is made even closer by one description of Huang Ti as being half snake, a creature who led the people out of the darkness of caves into the light. Nu Kua, successor and sister of Fu Hsi, was similarly seen as having the body of a snake and the head of a human. Huang Ti went to the four points of the compass, Yao sent emissaries there, Shun went to the four gates of the city. Huang Ti established the order for the sun, the moon and the stars. Yao charged his ministers to observe the Heavens and apply the law of numbers to the Sun, the Moon and the Constellations. The Five Sovereigns were not father and son to each other but rather sages selected to rule by their predecessors. This was the era of perfect rule. Yao banished his son so as not to be seen as showing favouritism. Filial piety and perfect rule are here recognized as being at odds with one another. The fact that filial piety remained the prime virtue of Emperor and commoner alike historically justified this principle.

The etymology of Huang (黃) – meaning yellow – is traditionally seen as resulting from the character for light, Kuang (光) being wrapped around the character for field T'ien (田).

The colour's primary reference is to the highly fertile loess which covers large areas of Northern China. Yellow is the imperial colour and as the Lord's place is in the centre so yellow is the colour of the central square of the Lo Shu magic square, the number of which is five. Since the Earth lies at the centre of the cosmological system, earth is the element associated with the central square. During feudal times the peasant communes divided their lands in accordance with the magic square and the produce from the central square was given to the Lord.

The Yellow Emperor is the deification of the earth, of the harvests, of the seasons and of the visible moving heavens that dictated the annual changes. The character for Yao (堯) breaks up into the decider of all the earth, the three earth characters representing the totality of earth.

Of the Five Sovereigns Huang Ti was first, followed by two sovereigns of no importance. Then came Yao followed by Shun – Shun was succeeded by Yu, who was also a sage; he had been chief of public works under Shun. He was descended from Huang Ti and the reason he was not the sixth sovereign is that he was succeeded by his son, so creating the first Royal dynasty – the Hsia dynasty.

Yu, too, ordered the world by visiting the 4 poles. His voice was the standard of sounds, his body the standard of measurement. He too tamed the mountains, dredged the marshes and fixed the rivers in their courses. The character Yu (禺) has the additional meaning of fullness and completion.

All dynasties rise and fall as the initial virtue that was inherent in the founder weakens with successive generations. That is the immutable law of dynasties. The Hsia rose and fell, to be replaced by the Yin (or Shang) which succumbed to the Chou. The war of succession between the Yin and the Chou is seen in almost cosmic terms. It was a war not only of men but of Gods. If a new God is created his story will be rooted in this conflict. When this happened in other mythologies it was usually a sign of two civilizations coming into conflict and resulting in one being subsumed into the other.

There appears to be evidence that two, both essentially Chinese, civilizations did exist. One in the East lived in marshy plains and were rice-growers. The other inhabited the West and were a civilization of terraces and of millet. The latter are said to have lived in caves. The

Yin were the rice-growers and the Chou the millet-reapers. It is very tempting, but no doubt erroneous, to see the origin of *Yin*, the female principle, and *Yang*, the male principle, as deriving from this opposition of two civilizations who nevertheless recognized a higher unity. (The two "Yins" are spoken with the same tone but their characters are different).

The earliest beliefs seem to fuse the ideas of the two civilizations. Huang Ti would have been a God of the West, of the loess region, but the constant reference to draining marshes shows a preoccupation which would been felt most keenly in the East.

Of a Hsia dynasty there is no archeological evidence. Prior to the the Yin and Shang cultures (It is not clear whether they were one or two cultures), there was only a series of tribal cultures dating from 5,000 BC. The Shang and Yin cultures arose at about the same time; 1,500 BC, in the three northern provinces of Shansi, Hopei and Shantung. The Shang seems to have first established the concept of a strong centralized power and the present word for "superior" is very similar in sound. Remains from this period show that all the north-south symbolism had already become established. The front doors of the Lords' Mansions faced South. Bodies were buried with the head to the North. When a lord died his entire retinue of wives and slaves as well as horses and such objects as would be of use to him in the next world were buried with him. In essence ancestor worship today is not too different, though wives are now spared.

The Chou, who fought and conquered the Shang, originated south of the Yellow river from present day Shansi and Honan. They overcame their neighbours and established the Chou dynasty in about 1027 BC.

The Chou "dynasty" was not extensive in territorial measurements. It probably covered some or most of Honan, Shantung, Shansi and Hopei. When it collapsed — and it was never a strong central power — China divided itself into states which were largely cut off from each other by barbarian peoples. This state of affairs existed for about 500 years until one of these states in an impressively rapid campaign, twelve years from 233 BC to 221 BC, conquered all the others and the Ch'in dynasty was created. It lasted only fifteen years but it changed China which now irrevocably entered its Imperial stage. It was at this time that the Great Wall of China was built.

The Ch'in gave way to the Han who maintained their control over the entire north of China. The South was not incorporated until the

T'ang dynasty (618–906 AD) which is why, even today, Chinese refer to themselves either as men of Han or men of T'ang. Chinatowns in foreign countries are *T'ang yang gai* (in Cantonese) meaning settlements of T'ang people. The South had in fact been conquered by the Ch'in but when that dynasty fell so did the fragile unity which was not to be resurrected for another 800 years.

Looking back over this stretch of history we see that the moment of the philosophers — of Confucius, Chuang Tzu, Mencius, Mo Tzu, Lieh Tzu, Han Fei and the countless, unnamed others — came at a time of extreme political unrest. The philosophies that arose were a direct response to this situation.

Each one was an attempt to provide a basis in reason for courses of action to be followed by the rulers. The philosophers looked to the rulers for their audience.

There were the Moralists who believed in goodness. Goodness involved right conduct — never expediency. If a king was good the people would be naturally attracted by his rule. The true king must observe the traditional rites with a pure heart. If the king acted thus so would the people. If society was at peace the heavens would remain in order and prosperity would result.

There were the Legalists who held that if each man were allowed to pursue his interest chaos would result. The only interest that should be allowed was that of the state. What was "right" was what the state wanted. To instil respect for this, they advocated comprehensive systems of punishment and reward. Only by doing this could the state become strong.

There were the Metaphysicists who believed that all actions inevitably created an equal, or stronger reaction. All actions were therefore futile. The king should rule by inaction. By this means he would create stillness at the centre. Peace would radiate but no one would know its source.

Only the Legalists really addressed themselves to the problem of attaining the ends already identified by the rulers, that is, of creating internal security and of conquering the neighbouring states. The history of Legalist domination has tended to confirm the Metaphysicists dictum of action and reaction. The Ch'in and the Sui dynasties were primarily Legalist states. The first lasted fifteen years, the second 29 years. Yet the brevity belies their importance. Both unified China after extended periods of conflict. The Great Wall was built during the first and the Grand Canal during the second. These ensured the survival and progress of China. The Legalists never disappeared and they are much admired. by the present Communist Goverment, itself essentially Legalist. The other two schools are of course much better known under the terms Confucianism and Taoism.

The Strange Case
of Confucius

Confucius is usually viewed either with antipathy as a dusty traditionalist or with immense respect for having laid down standards of morality and behaviour. Revered by scholars and bureaucrats, he was ridiculed by Taoists and despised by Legalists. The present People's Republic of China has denounced Confucianism but this is not because there has suddenly sprung up a "back to the trees" diehard radical Confucianist movement. Confucianism is merely a handy label to slap on any traditional virtue that stands in the way of communist progress — revering one's father before the state, for example.

In the other Republic of China the Confucian cult retains its imperial vigour and celebrations attending his festival are televised. A black ox is sacrificed in his honour and for days after men and women can be found searching the flagstones in the hope of finding a hair of the victim. Sentiments in this matter are still strong.

These extremes of reverence and revulsion for the ideas he put forward are evidence enough of their potency. Whereas the Legalists addressed themselves to answering the political problems of the princes and the Taoists' ideas were directed at the alienated and dispossessed, Confucius addressed himself to society. He gave the first written expression of the morality already implicit in the culture in which he lived. By formalizing these moral precepts, he created a philosophical armoury for the rising class of bureaucrats against the self-seeking excesses of the ruling cliques. He stood at the centre of a power struggle and this perhaps explains his severity of tone. Perhaps it was his high-minded seriousness that inevitably led to his becoming the butt of jokes — Confucius jokes have a long history! The following two stories show something of their flavour.

One day a disciple of Confucius asked the music master Chiu what he thought of his master's ideas.

"It is finished," said Chiu.

"Why do you say that?" asked the disciple.

"If you disturb the dead you will assuredly suffer from evil dreams. Confucius was thrown out of Wei, reduced to starvation in Sung, near death in Chou, were these not bad dreams?"

"Again, if you are travelling by sea you use a boat, if by land you use a carriage. To seek or practise the ways of Chou in Lu is like pushing a boat across dry land."

"If you dress a monkey in the robes of a duke, it will bite and tear until he is rid of them. The difference between antiquity and the present time is as great as between the monkey and the duke."

"Alas, it is all over with your master."

A more scurrilous example is this:

"There were two brothers, one of whom was a sage. The other was a brigand who lived by pillage and rape. Confucius told the sage to talk to his brother and bring him to the path of morality. When the sage demurred, Confucius took it to himself to go. When he arrived he prostrated himself on the ground and said that having heard of his (the brigand Chih's) Excellency as a champion of morality he had come to pay his respects. Brigand Chih refused to see him saying "why, this is that crafty fraud from Lu . . . (who) dresses up in a forked hat that looks as though a tree had taken root in his head, puts the whole flank of a dead ox around his belly and then chatters unceasingly, heaping nonsense upon nonsense . . . wags his lips and drums his tongue . . . deluding all the rulers under Heaven with his private notion of right and wrong . . . pretends to be interested only in filial piety and brotherly obedience, but spends his time currying favour with landed lords, with the rich and great. Tell the fellow that he is a scoundrel for whom no punishment would be too great, and if he doesn't clear out of here at once, we shall add his liver to our morning stew."

Finally admitted to the brigand's presence, Confucius attempts flattery after flattery and not only fails in his attempt but barely escapes with his life.

Most of the other stories put Confucius in the role of the hapless intellectual whose fate it is to be routed in argument by every Taoist he meets.

All this is very unfair to Confucius whose personal bravery should not be so impugned.

Confucius was born in the state of Lu, southern Shantung, in 552 BC. He died in 479 BC. He is credited with having held ministerial positions in that state, the highest being Prime Minister. It is equally likely that he held none at all. He spent some years travelling from state to state and finally returned to Lu, where he spent the last three years of his life writing and instructing students.

To explain his leaving Lu, after a supposedly successful ministerial life, the story is told that under his guidance the state of Lu grew strong and powerful, so much so that the neighbouring states became afraid and, in order to distract the Prince of Lu from the practice of government, sent him a troupe of dancing girls. They must have been very attractive for he was distracted. Confucius left in disgust and went in search of a righteous Lord to whom he would become minister. In this he failed. After twelve years of wandering he returned to Lu and, according to tradition, wrote the classics.

The story of the dancing girls is also told in a different context. Confucius saved his Prince from an ambush by girl dancers while on a state visit to Ch'i. Confucius had arranged for a large escort so there was no danger. He berated the Duke of Ch'i for using barbarian methods and the duke was suitably humbled.

Stories of sword dancers being used to get rid of guests are common enough in literature and may very well stem from real incidents. In both these stories the role of the dancing girls is dangerous to the Prince.

On the subject of music, Confucius is said to have abstained from meat for three months after listening to a piece of music, exclaiming, "I did not imagine that music could be made so perfect."

Confucius has come down to us as a dried out pleasure-hater. Yet one of the classics attributed to him was the Music Classic. He himself played the lute. He was not against pleasure. "Use poetry to arouse the good in men. Use ritual to give it form. Use music to set it in harmonious motion." But the pleasure he advocated was a very sedate kind of pleasure.

If he himself never held office the stories of the dancing girls are suspect, yet no story of Confucius' life is complete without them. Why are they so important? When Confucius and other sages wished to make a point they did so by telling a story which illustrated it. The idea of dancing girls is most evocative and would ensure interest. Both stories illustrate in different ways the misuse of princely power. Harmony in society depended on the benevolence and wisdom of the ruler. This is a basic tenet of Confucianism. If I am right, these stories are simply evocative expressions of this philosophy. It may also be the case that Confucian ideas of pleasure being bound up with harmony may not have extended to dancing girls, who were themselves probably free with their sexual favours and whose dances were certainly not all slow and decorous.

Confucius lived at a time of the warring feudal states. These states needed administrators to take charge of the day to day administration. It was his belief that these states should be wholly governed by men whose superiority lay in their wisdom and intelligence and not in family ties. In this he was most democratic. His ideal was a bureaucracy of righteous men, who manipulated traditional rites and customs to create an harmonious state which did not lean heavily on its citizens.

The need to organize and administer increases with the size and complexity of the state. Bureaucracy was unavoidable and clearly the strain was beginning to be felt at this time (500 BC). The feudal hierarchy had to appoint administrators from the lower orders. These administrators, hampered by feudal constraints, began 'to see new possibilities. It is more than likely that Confucius did hold office and belonged to this frustrated generation. Persuasion or violence were the only means to attain the necessary change. Confucius preached, others rebelled. Legend has it that Confucius was twice tempted to join rebels who wished to impose a bureaucratic state (source of the brigand Chih story).

Confucius saw himself as having a mission. At a time when human life was cheap he confronted princes and dukes more or less tactfully, with denunciations. These now appear to be rather pedantic homilies — but this is only because his vision of the future was inevitable and when it came into being was quickly taken for granted. Confucius stood on the battle line and the charge of cowardice must be withdrawn. The fact that he was listened to and survived suggests he was imposing and not without charm.

His bureaucratic rationalism was compounded by a sentimentality for tradition. He would have liked the ancient ritual observances to be resurrected — an attitude only possible if one separated their operational effect in relation to the other world from their effect on the participants in this. Confucius did not concern himself with the other world, only with this one. His sentimentality is nicely recorded in an exchange with his students. He asked them what they most wished they could do. Two wanted ministerial control of domains, one to become a ritual specialist but the last said that he would wish to take part in the ancient dance of spring between grown men and boys on the banks of a river. Clearly this rite was no longer performed. Confucius sighed and agreed that he too would have wished for this.

By advocating the resurrection of rites fallen out of use because they no longer had meaning, it was inevitable that a purely ritualistic formalism would take over. Confucius, a revolutionary, became, simply because his thought was an expression of a necessary process, the archetype of conservatism. He did not help his image by being a traditionalist in his own time. In connection with his obsession with filial piety — which clearly was not his invention — it is worth telling the story of his birth as it has come down to us. Confucius' father only had one son who was lame. In order to conduct the sacrifices to the ancestors one had to be whole. At the age of seventy or more, to fulfil his duty as a son, he remarried — and Confucius was the product of that union.

People talk of Confucianism as a religion — unfettered by the problem that his philosophical statements were uniformly this-world in nature; it is recorded that there were four subjects on which he refused to talk — extraordinary things, unnatural strength, natural disasters and spiritual beings, his Tao was the Tao of society.

On his death a cult grew up. A shrine was erected to his memory and a cult, in all ways resembling an ancestor cult, was established. It remained a private cult restricted to his family and to self-proclaimed Confucians. It wasn't until 195 BC that the first emperor come to worship here, not until 37 AD that the family was ennobled and not until 59 AD that the Emperor Han Ming Ti ordered sacrifices to be made to him in all the schools in the country. These schools were only established the previous year. It was this act that made him a state deity.

Until this time his worship was a family affair and his temple was the ancestral hall of the Kung family. An ancestral hall contains the plaques with the names of the ancestors of a family. We must assume that the Kung family ancestral hall was unique in one respect — that, long before official recognition was given, it also contained the plaques of his disciples. The hall therefore functioned in two ways. Official recognition involved a separation of these functions for Confucian temples, usually built on the model of a palace — a *kung* (although it is called *miao*) — contain the plaque of Confucius in the central shrine and around the walls the plaques of recognized disciples — not family. The number of these disciples is open to increase by Imperial edict. The last two were added in 1919 — though this fact should be interpreted as a preliminary statement of Imperial intentions on the part of certain warlords, notably Chang Tso-lin, at that time for, of course, in

1919 there was no emperor.

No one is very clear on the dates of the next phase — it may have happened gradually — but it became compulsory, probably during the Han dynasty, for temples to be set up in every administrative district in the empire from the level of the province down to the sub-prefecture. The unimportance of Hong Kong can be seen from the absence of any such temple.

Confucius gradually climbed up an hierarchical ladder. Imperial decrees made him a Duke, a King and in 1106 AD an emperor. Subsequently he was made Perfectly Holy Ancient Master. The absence of other titles is seen as the highest honour that could be paid to him.

It is not a coincidence that the spring and autumn equinoxes mark the major celebrations of Confucius. These days designated the division of the year in ancient times. The spring equinox inaugurated ploughing and the planting of seed. It was also the signal for love and betrothal. The bursting into blossom of flowers at this time has made them the universal gift of love and this was no less true in ancient China. Autumn was the season of harvests and marriage. Spring was the festival of the young, autumn of the old. Social harmony depends on the harmony of the season; and the harmony of the universe — and thus of the seasons — is dependent on the harmonious conduct of society. Heaven and Earth are bound together in the flux of the universe. Confucius is the guardian of stability in the internal workings of the state. He is the guardian of social harmony. Thus we see the concepts of the peasant preserved and established in the orthodoxy of the state.

Some authorities have suggested that Confucius is not a God. Their argument is that in the order of supernatural beings he is not a *shen* but a *kuei*, i.e. not of the higher but of the lower order. The point here is an interesting one and must be balanced against the fact that Imperial edicts gave him the titles "Ancestral Saint" and "Accomplished and Illustrious Prince." — given in 1370 AD by the emperor Ch'eng Tsung. The translation of *Sheng* as Saint is appropriate for our purposes, though "Holy One" might be a more exact equivalent, for in the western church saints are worshipped but are not Gods. In the West we admit of only one God and thus we can make the distinction absolute. This is not the case in China where the number of Gods is potentially infinite. There is no Chinese word equivalent to our word "God". Westerners have assumed that the category *shen* covers much the same spectrum of meaning. I suggest it does not.

There is a remarkable similarity between the cult of Confucius and the cult of the Earth Gods. As they both operate in a territorial manner, it is hard to escape the conclusion that Confucius is the Earth God of the state. The Earth Gods might better be called Territory Gods. Each house has one, each neighbourhood, each village. Historically, when towns and cities arose, the city God became the pre-eminent Earth God of the locality. It is a hierarchy of Gods which demarcates the functioning units of society. If one goes to any village one will see at the entrance a stone block on which joss-sticks have been placed. This is the Earth God of the village.

One village near Yuen Long, of some age, can be approached by three paths crossing a stream. At the village end of each path stands a shrine to an Earth God. Only one is well-kept and that stands on the most frequently used path. They are acting as the village Door Gods.

While the village has its Earth Gods so too does each household. Even more than the village the house represents a microcosm of the universe and its protection is of prime importance. The array of protective devices is correspondingly more complex. Above the door there is often a mirror to keep at bay evil spirits, at the foot of the door there is usually a plaque made of wood or tin to the Earth God of the door. Half way up the door frame there will be a plaque again of wood or tin to the Sky God. The Door God invokes wealth, the Sky God invokes happiness.

At the centre of the house there is another tablet usually facing the door but on the ground. This is the most complete invocation of wealth to be found. Roughly translated character for character it reads from top to bottom, right to left:

ground	front	five	Earth
can	back	points	can
give	Earth	five	create
yellow	owner	earths	white
gold	money	dragon	jade
	god	god	

Another God of the household, the God of the Stove, looks over the destiny of the family and reports to Heaven at the end of every year. As a family is defined by the communal use of the same stove we can understand why this God has the functions he does. Here the plaque translates as: constant happiness Stove God. These all seem to be the permanent aspects of these Gods but there is an annual aspect involving paper images. Those of the Kitchen God and the God of Wealth are ceremoniously burnt and then replaced on New Year's afternoon. On the outside doors two red-faced generals one dressed in red the other in black are pasted up to guard the entrance. They are soon reduced to tatters by the elements but this does not seem to weaken their efficacy for they are only replaced once a year.

Earth Gods are often called True Gods of Good Fortune and Virtue. The provision of good fortune and the maintenance of virtue are their other duties. Most Earth Gods of neighbourhoods and larger units have cut into them the characters *Fu* (福), *Lu* (祿) and *Shou* (壽). Happiness, High rank and Long life. I don't think that it is wholly coincidental that there is a correspondence of sounds with *Fu* meaning boundary, *Lu* meaning village gate, *Lu* meaning path and *Shou* meaning to guard.

Confucius is the "Earth" god of the state but whereas the worship of Earth Gods is the function of the community, the worship of Confucius is the function of officials and Literati.

Confucianism has often been called a religion. In view of what has gone before, I think it is clear that this is a misconception. Confucius is a "God" but not in his own religion. He is a patron God of the bureaucracy and of academics and the Earth God of the state.

The Problem of Lao Tzu

Books on Taoism usually suffer from the fervour of the fellow traveller. We are, they seem to tell us, face to face with TRUTH. Unfortunately this truth has to be interpreted. What we are too often confronted with is an interpretation of a book — the *Tao Te Ching*. Other aspects of Taoism — such as the inconvenient fact that it incorporates a religion with Gods and priests — tend to be ignored. When this fact isn't ignored it is assumed that the religion stemmed from the teachings — it didn't.

Taoism in all its forms — philosophical, religious, alchemical, nutritional etc., — gives great weight to the book *Tao Te Ching*. However only the first movement can really be said to have arisen as a result of the book. The other elements of Taoism attached themselves to the book as they developed. They were able to do this because the book is unrivalled in its obscurity. Thus, for instance, when the book talks of the "realized man" some could see in this a reference to an immortal.

The *Tao Te Ching* is traditionally ascribed to Lao Tzu and it is worth saying a few words about him. I say "a few words" advisedly for there is little to tell. There is, in the *Tao Te Ching*, a line that goes: "As to the Sage, no one will know if he existed or not". This is most apt given the search for the author. It is not just a matter of not knowing when he existed but if he existed at all. Clearly the *Tao Te Ching* was written by somebody, though not necessarily one person. It has been dated as not earlier than 400 BC. Unfortunately most legends place Lao Tzu in the sixth century BC.

Let us start with one legend. A woman was fertilized by a falling star and after a gestation period of 62 years she leant against a plum tree and gave birth to a white-haired baby who could speak. He pointed to the plum tree and took his surname from it *Li* and then fingered his ear and feeling that it was large he took as his personal name *Erh* (ear). He was born on the 14 September 604 BC in the Kingdom of Chou, lived 160 years during which time he held the post of Keeper of the Archives at Loyang, and then disgusted with the corruption at court, mounted a black ox and left the Middle Kingdom. As he went through the Han Ku Pass the keeper of the pass begged him to write down something of his thoughts. He agreed to do so and with 5,000 characters composed the *Tao Te Ching.*

When Ssu-ma Chien, the first Chinese historian, came to write Lao Tzu's biography he very quickly threw his hands up in frustration. What few details there were contradicted each other. He was not born in 604 BC but 571 BC, the gestation lasted not 62 years but 81 years; he was born not in the Kingdom of Chou but in Ch'in. Ssu-ma Chien was a Confucian and Confucians have always classed numerology, *fung-sui* and other such manifestations as superstitions: Western scholars seem to have followed this attitude and for this reason have failed to see the purely mythological character of Lao Tzu. To understand this we have to refer both to the magic square and to *fung-sui.*

Let us first look at the curious exactness of the date. The 14 September is almost certainly the Autumn Moon Festival which in Chinese reckoning is the fifteenth day of the eighth moon. If we look at the magic square this places him in the hall numbered seven, on either side are six and two; sixty-two was the length of his mother's pregnancy. The calendrical sign for September is the city gate. Autumn relates to the compass direction west. In the second version of the story the length of pregnancy is given as 81 years. Eight and one are the numbers of the last two halls of winter. The last hall of winter is associated with mountains and gate-keepers and its animal sign is the ox. Lastly 14 September lies in the solar period — of which there are 24 to a year — "white dew" — we remember that he was born with white hair.

The Autumn Moon Festival is the Harvest festival and has always been a time of feasting and drinking. It is the festival that marks the growing strength of the female principle that rules the world until spring when the male principle again becomes ascendant. At this time of the year — sometimes on the same day as the Moon Festival — the Star Gods of Wealth and Longevity are also worshipped.

Let us turn now to the years of his birth 604 BC and 571 BC. Clearly this method of stating the year is of Western origin. The Chinese normally stated the year in terms of the emperor reigning at the time. They also had, and still have, a method based on cycles of sixty years. Each year has a name composed of two words. The first is the celestial stem, the second the terrestrial branch. The first repeats itself in cycles of ten, the second in cycles of twelve. The year 604 BC would have been the year *Ting Ssu*; 571 BC would have been *Keng Yin*.

Ting Ssu has the meaning of "to sustain sons" while *Keng Yin* contains strong implications of the need for radical improvement: *Keng* (age, change, reward) and *Yin* (illness, treat well).

We see a complementary set of ideas when we examine the names by which he is known; Li Erh, Lao Tzu and Lao Tan. Li means plum tree and this plant is associated with long life and the north (winter). Erh, the ear, is the part of the body relating to the north. Lao Tzu has the associations of a) Lao: old, autumn and b) Tzu — one of the terrestial branches: mid-winter, death, official position and wisdom. Tan (聃) breaks down into ear and remedy. He is only known by the name Lao Tan when he is said to be working in the official Archives as keeper. These archives were the repository of the lore of divination, magical prayers, and of astral, medical and pharmaceutical science. In this capacity he would have been one of the divinatory and ritual experts of the Emperor.

Let us now return to that part of the story where he leaves the capital city, Loyang, and quits the empire through the west gate. The gate-keeper in the story is sufficiently important for his name to have come down to us. It is either Yin Hsi, Ruler of Joy or Kuan Yin-tzu, Master Ruler of the Gate. Who is this ruler of Joy at the west gate? The most likely candidate is the Queen of Western Heaven, belief in whom is of some antiquity, fifth century BC at least. She was formed by the conjunction of Heaven and Earth and thus she presides over all life and therefore over death. The idea of long life was bound up with the concept of virtue. If one lived to old age this was proof of one's virtue. Her temple in Peking is situated in the N.E. of the city — that is to say in the hall whose number is eight and whose animal sign is the ox. This hall is the seat of the Greater Female principle. According to the history of the Chou dynasty the Emperor Mu entertained her in 985 BC. This story would have been spread to show that heavenly favour had been bestowed on the dynasty.

Each dynasty ruled and continued to rule only because on it had been bestowed the Virtue of Heaven. At the beginning of each dynasty the virtue is strong but as emperor follows emperor the virtue of the dynasty weakens until there comes a point when the virtue is transferred to another who starts a new dynasty. The proof of virtue is success. In the time Lao Tzu is placed, the Chou dynasty was beginning to come apart. Though in theory it lasted until 221 BC the period 481–211 BC is called the period of the Warring States. By 500 BC the empire had fragmented and power lay in the hands of the feudal lords. On this point the story is quite explicit. Lao Tzu left Loyang in disgust with the corruption of the empire. If the story, taken as a whole means anything it is this: the Chou Emperors had been invested with the Virtue of Heaven. This virtue had run out. Lao Tzu is the embodiment of that virtue departing from the Empire. This is emphasized by the fact that he rode a black ox. The ox is an emblem of spring because to inaugurate the spring and bring an end to winter a black ox was sacrified. There are two possible references here. Either the ox has been sacrified to usher in the spring of a new dynasty or, as I prefer it, the sacrifice has walked off. There will be no new spring until the dynasty ends. If the rites are not performed chaos is inevitable. The idea of sacrifice gains some support from the fact that the word for this is Erh (衈) blood + ear. If the virtue had left to whom had it been transferred? Clearly there are opposing claims. In one version the virtue was born in the Kingdom of Ch'in and the other posits the Kingdom of Chou. When the Chou dynasty broke up into overlordships, four of them became powerful: Ch'i, Chou, Ch'in and Chin. Of these Chou and Ch'in gradually brought their claims to notice but at the time referred to in the myth they were not the most powerful. We are however dependant for our information on Ssu-ma Chien who lived much later (145–86 BC). It is not the balance of power in 604 BC or 571 BC that counts but that which later materialized and this was a very even balance between these two kingdoms. Chou was on the brink of founding – or re-consolidating – the Empire when they were defeated by Ch'in. The myths of Lao Tzu are the competing myths of two kingdoms fighting for the prize of Imperial suzerainty.

However the story does not end here. The immense associational wealth of the myth of Lao Tzu (which can mean Master Lao but also Venerable Seed) created, as we have seen, a dark spirit whose sphere of influence covered the dead end of the year. He was thus opposed to the God of Spring and of the Harvest Huang Ti. They opposed but they also complemented each other and around 200 BC a composite figure emerged: Huang Lao-chun. This God governed the world but did not interfere with it. In 165 AD he was worshipped as the creator of the world and later on became subsumed into a new divinity T'ien Tsun, Celestial Honoured Being. Lao Tzu seems to have retained his own distinct personality, for in 666 AD the Emperor Kao Tsung made him

"Great Supreme Emperor of Dark Supreme Cause."

None of the foregoing clarifies the issue of who wrote the *Tao Te Ching* — but that is a quite separate problem. The idea that Lao Tzu wrote it at the Han Ku Pass was perhaps suggested by the name of that pass which can either mean "contain ravine" or "letter to nourish." The purely mythological reality of Lao Tzu becomes irrefutable when we discover that Lao Tzu was not originally the name of a man but the original title of the book he is supposed to have written: the *Tao Te Ching*.

Nature Cults,
Alchemists and Gods

The early Taoists lived up to their belief that harmony and knowledge can only radiate from a still centre and the man who wrote the *Tao Te Ching* has clearly lived up to this. The book is as abstruse in meaning as it is in origin and those who wish to follow it up can do so elsewhere. Here I will simply say that the book gives expression to the idea that before Heaven and Earth existed there was a something which was without attributes:

It's true name we do not know.

"Way" is the by name that we give it.

But this something gave rise to two forces: *Tao* and *Te*. Of these two forces *Tao* is the less knowable. *Tao* might be equated with the power behind being and *Te* the power behind action.

Those who took the book as a guide addressed themselves not primarily — or even secondarily — to the state but to existence itself. They were, in fact, anti-state. Many turned to an hermetic existence, others to a primitive communalism which rejected labour saving devices. Behind both choices was a desire to subsume self into the unity and spontaneity of nature. We shall call these people philosophical Taoists. The Taoism they followed seems to me to have been an intellectualization of the unsystematized conceptions of the ancient peasantry. Whereas Confucius had a sentimental approach to the forms of peasant life, the philosophical Taoists wished to re-create that life.

Alongside these communalist ideas there was also a belief in the possibility of immortality. These ideas were generally not held by the purely philosophical schools who often attacked them. Yet this idea that it was possible must have been deep-rooted for it took a strong hold. In 400 BC an expedition was sent to sea to look for the mushroom of immortality. The belief only died (or was it that it took on another shape?) with the rise of beliefs in personalized Gods.

These would-be immortals used various techniques to attain their ends. There were respiratory techniques which involved attempting to live on one's own breath by swallowing balls of saliva; heliotherapeutic techniques which involved lying naked under the sun for men, and under the moon for women; gymnastic techniques which have come down to us as T'ai Chi and Kung Fu; sexual techniques which often involved orgies (the union of breaths) and appear to have involved semen retention; pharmaceutical techniques — the making and taking of elixirs and, lastly, dietary techniques — abstention from grain for example.

Spitting, T'ai Chi, the taking of virility pills, the care given to food and drink — all are common aspects of present day life and behind them lie a sense of the importance of health. One cannot write about the Chinese without constantly referring to "harmony". Disease and ill-health are disturbers of harmony. The filial son does nothing that is likely to cause himself injury for he must be whole if he is to participate in the ancestral rites. What is immortality except the retention, forever, of a healthy body?

The Alchemists, Hygienists and the Philosophical Taoists all, one way or another, traced their descent from the great Taoist Sages. There was another element which became incorporated into the Taoist stream and its importance has always been underestimated. This element was not an intellectual school and for that reason it tended to be written off. It did not fit into the scheme of a purely mentalist approach to history. Before the arrival of the Taoists, the religious specialists were magicians or "sorcerers" of one sort or another. It was the incorporation of these people, their ideas, beliefs and practices that gave Taoism the element crucial to the formation of a religion.

We have seen that the idea of the gate entailed danger and the need for protection. A system that strives for harmony is a closed system — disruption to such a system can only come from outside. Each house is a system striving for harmony and the fact that doors are breaches in the system make them dangerous. One type of sorcerer was the Hsien-men. He went into trances and journeyed to the land of the dead. Here he communed with the spirits and through them he was able to foretell the future. As the living and the dead occupy different systems it is no surprise to find the idea of a gate involved. Hsien-men literally means "longed for (or desired) gate". These sorcerers also made the sacrifices to the mountains and rivers, invoked rain, worked cures and used bones to divine the future. They are more commonly referred to as Shamans.

Another type of sorcerer was the Wu, who similarly went into trances and mingled with the spirits. The Wu were generally women and dancing was one of their basic practices. It seems that the dancing girls who did not endear themselves to Confucius were Wu and that these dances were not simply displays but were enacted to create contact with the world of the dead. In the province of Shantung, i.e. the Kingdom of Lu, Confucius' home, and portions of the neighbouring states, the eldest daughter of every family was considered a Wu and for that reason not allowed to marry. Whether their virginity was strictly enforced or whether they were, in the environment of the court, free with their favours is not known. It is tempting to believe the latter for coupling with a Wu must have entailed a sense of coupling with the spirits of the other world. Sexual union cannot be separated from the idea of life and later Taoist ideas of the female orgasm strengthening men's vital powers were very likely of ancient origin. Such union with a Wu would have reinforced this efficacy. It is worth noting that the words for female orgasm, ghosts*, tortoise shell, and menses* have much the same sound, those asterisked being now identical. The tortoise shell was used for divination.

Wu have not disappeared, nor have ecstatic performances. The annual festival at the temple to Monkey in Sau Mau Ping in Kowloon, Hong Kong, involves trances – but by a male medium. Present day Taoist priests are always men and, while they don't go into trances, they do dance.

The Fang-shih were different. The term is often translated as "Gentlemen possessing magical recipes" (or "formulas" in the chemical sense).

An independant movement of "elixir" believers appeared around 200 BC and one of them was the first recorded alchemist. These were the Fang-shih. However, it is also possible to translate "Fang" as "square" thus making the term mean "gentleman who understands the square." Now this may be purely coincidental or it may point to a blending of two different roles for there is one type of "sorcerer" who so far has not appeared in the discussion. This is the ritual expert whose profession created the magic square and much of the meaning now involved in the science of *Fung-sui.* This sorcerer may have been a Hsien-men. Before the arrival of the Taoists the religious specialists were magicians or sorcerers of one sort or another. It was the incorporation of these people, their concepts and their practices that gave Taoism the element crucial to the formation of a religion.

These "sorcerers" have a long history. King Li (d.828 BC) employed them to "close the people's mouths". Unfortunately little is known of this office or the functions of the office holders yet it is these people who created what system of meaning there is underlying much of Chinese thought.

As ritual becomes complex, it becomes specialized. As it increases in complexity it can no longer be left to the head of a clan. As life becomes more complex so does the ritual that attends it. Ritual occurs not only at the times of the special communal acts but relates to all social intercourse. With the rise of the feudal lord, the Lord, as Son of Heaven, was particularly exposed to the danger of making an inappropriate ritual act. To show this I will turn to an example given by Granet in "The Religion of the Chinese People".

"A minor lord is visiting a powerful one; the latter dies; the ministers want to force the guest to dress the corpse: that is to dishonour him, to treat him as a vassal. If he obeys, he gives up his sovereign independance; and how could he not obey? His own vassals first try to refuse, then find an answer: their lord proceeds to the dressing, but he brings a sorcerer with him; it was thus that a prince acted in his own estates when he paid a visit of condolence to a vassal. In that way, the situation is completely transformed: the humiliation rebounds upon the presumptuous domain."

This story tells us not only of the dangers, but also of the fact that each lord had a "sorcerer". This ritual expert was only one of many — there were experts in the military arts, in astrology, in economy and in law, among others.

So much for its various constituent parts but history intervenes and spurs Taoism on its way. The events about to be described started about 150 AD. The Han Emperors were no longer in control of the empire and, their virtue was running out. Control was reverting to the feudal lords. At such times the world seems out of balance and the peasantry were as much affected as everyone else.

In Szechuan a man named Chang Ling started a health cult which involved "miracle" cures. The cult grew in popularity. The charge for a cure was an annual payment of five pecks of rice. He was a Shaman but he also had a doctrine, which he expounded and published, based on the *Tao Te Ching*. His interpretation of this book was rather curious; so the first line of the book which is literally "The *Tao* that can be *Tao*-ed" means good things should be eaten in the morning and "The *Tao* that is not eternal" means to have bowel movements in the evening.

We have here a blending of nutritionism, philosophical Taoism and Shamanism. As we shall see the shamanistic element remains dominant. But all this would have been merely of curiosity value if he hadn't done something new. He created an organization. This was dictated by circumstances. Implicit in the idea of dues is the collection of these dues. He appointed officers who were also healers and took to himself the title Celestial Master (T'ien Shih). The idea of collecting dues in the first place may very well have come from Buddhist missionaries who had been arriving in China for a century or more.

The cult gradually attained theological control over a sizeable territory and obtained influence with the governor of the region. This resulted in the grandson of Chang Ling, Chang Lu, being given an army to attack, successfully, an enemy of the governor's. In this campaign Chang Lu was helped by a general called Chang Hsiu (no relation). This Chang Hsiu was a warlord who likewise had organized a health cult of his own. He may have been inspired in this by Chang Ling's cult or it may suggest the wide spread and acceptance of the same fundamental ideas. Chang Hsiu's cures were obtained by imprisoning the ill to think over their sins. The patient then wrote down his sins on three pieces of paper — one was exposed on a mountain top, one buried in the earth and one cast to the waters. The idea of sin shows a much stronger Buddhist influence. His hierarchy was militaristic as well as religious — converts being called demon soldiers.

Chang Hsiu must have been highly astute for it is clear that the development of society had so advanced that the Lord was largely cut off from the people. The Lord could no longer rely on them to do one's bidding. Chang Hsiu aimed at their hearts and minds. He was not however astute enough for after several campaigns his "partner" Chang Lu had him executed and took over his cult. This he did just after occupying a mountainous prefecture in the north, Han-chung.

Chang Lu now set up a theocratic state which he held for 30 years before surrendering to Ts'ao Ts'ao, a ruthless but highly capable minister who totally dominated the last Han Emperor, and whose son became the next Emperor. Chang Lu was given a fief. This was in Kiangsi province. He or one of his descendants built a palace there in the Dragon-Tiger Mountains. They remained there until the communist take-over and in western literature they are referred to as the Taoist Popes. To have survived for so long suggests that they renounced their militaristic aspects. These were lifted to the ideal plane.

We must now return to the beginnings, for there was another movement in many respects identical to Chang Ling's on the other side of China, in Shantung. This movement was led by still another Chang; Chang Chueh. It is unlikely that he was a relation of Chang Lu but the debate continues as a proven relationship would explain the extent of the similarities. He too set up an organization based on the Five Pecks of Rice, as those in Szechuan were known, and its militaristic motif is evident in Chang Chueh's title "Celestial General".

In 175 AD he sent out eight apostles, one to each province, and by 184 most of these provinces had become converted to the Tao of Grand Peace. The speed of their success must be explained by the sharp increases in taxation necessary to support the excesses of the eunuchs and the fact that crops were failing. There were famines and epidemics. A Health Cult can thus be seen as the obvious expression of people who were underfed and who could see, or certainly feel, in the emptiness of their stomachs, the imminent collapse of the state.

In 184 the Central Government decided to check the growth of this movement but the sect leaders were warned. On one day 360,000 men put yellow sashes round their heads and the Yellow Turban Rebellion was launched. Chang Chueh and his brothers were executed that same year but for the next twenty years, the Yellow Turbans were still a substantial military problem. This rising destroyed the Empire and contributed to the partitioning of the country into the three kingdoms. The church hierarchy was not destroyed. The leaders continued to function as priests and the organization gradually coalesced with Chang Lu's sect. This fusion was slow and a centralized authority was never more than theoretical. When monasteries and parishes came into existence each had its own hierarchy. The Tao-shih, the priest who officiated at ceremonies, either lived in a monastery or in the village. The office was hereditary. Nowadays these Tao-shih usually manage "God shops" where incense, paper talismans and funeral offerings can be bought. They are not usually connected with temples.

The Taoist pantheon of Gods had not yet been formulated. At first they took over and accepted as their own the religious beliefs of the time so that now to talk of Taoism as a religion is at one level to talk of the ancient indigenous beliefs of the people. On top of these beliefs they erected an hierarchy of immortals, aping the Buddhist concept of the Arhat. The comprehensiveness of the Buddhist theology with which they were competing spurred the Taoists into creating their own systems which in many respects were modelled on that of the rivals.

Whereas the philosophical Taoists continued in their anti-state posture, the religious Taoist, or at least those who were closer to the Alchemists and Fang-shih, were bound up in the ritual of the state and were necessarily pro-state. This coupled with the ancient belief in the unity of Heaven and Earth resulted in a conception of Heaven which Waley, in his introduction to "Monkey", describes so well.

"The idea that the hierarchy in Heaven is a replica of government on earth is an accepted one in China. Here as so often the Chinese let the cat out of the bag, where other countries leave us guessing. It has often been put forward as a theory that a people's gods are a replica of its earthly rulers. In most, cases the derivation is obscure. But in the Chinese popular belief there is no ambiguity. Heaven is simply the "whole bureaucratic system transferred bodily to the empyrean."

There are ministries governing every aspect of life from time of birth to manner of death. Nevertheless it must not be imagined that somewhere there is written down the entire list of ministries and the names of the Gods in charge of these ministries. Nothing is ever that simple. We are talking about an assumption. If a ministry is important then the God will be named. Gods are occasionally demoted and promoted but this generally happens at the lowest level, at that of the City God, whose position was often as tenuous as that of the magistrate who was his terrestrial equivalent. The City God, lowest Heavenly operative and highest Earth God, is the link between this religion — sometimes called the official religion — and the religion of the people.

An interesting aspect of this religion is that there was no concept of an all-pervasive God who knew all the details of one's actions. On the contrary the supreme God was immensely distanced from the details of existence. He relied on agents, the God of the Stove for the household and the City God for the bureaucracy, to go to his palace once a year, at the new year, to report on the doings on earth. If further illustration is needed of the similarity of the official religion with the ancient religion we need only consider the God of the Stove, more commonly known as the Kitchen God.

In the eighth century BC there existed a belief that Heaven looked down on those below, kept a record of men's doings, and accordingly judged how many years to bestow on individuals. Long life was the reward of virtue. By the sixth century Heaven had become more distanced and the work was undertaken by an agent called the Director of Destinies. He was the God usually invoked by Shamans.

The first record in which the Director of Destinies is clearly associated with the stove is the report that Li Shao Chun, considered to be the first alchemist, insisted that it was necessary for the success of a venture to pray to the God of the Stove. This was in 133 BC.

In early feudal times the clan was the centre of man's interest. All men of the father's generation were called father. One did not accord one's own father more respect than his brother. As China developed and towns and cities grew up the cohesion of the commune collapsed and gradually men's interests centred more on their own immediate household than on the village as a whole. One accorded to one's father the respect that, previously, had only been bestowed on the head of the clan. Heaven responds to changes in society. The integration of the Director of Destinies into the household is a reflection of this fragmenting of the old commune.

It is possible that the science of alchemy rose out of this association. If one accorded the God of the Stove (the Kitchen God) great respect and heated on the stove compounds of the utmost purity, could one not then be able to extend one's span? Whether or not this was the origin of alchemical concepts, the idea that one can affect the annual report of one's conduct is enshrined in the practice of offering the God sweet food, prior to his departure, in order to sweeten his words. The Chinese know their officials and their penchant for sweeteners.

There is an obvious correlation between the rise of personified Gods and the creation of the Imperial State. Under the state system men could rise to the top echelons of the bureaucracy through their own efforts, so it was in the Heavenly Ministries.

In a manner similar to canonization by the Catholic Church men were raised, to certain positions, usually but not always, low down in the hierarchy – particularly to the offices of City God. Conversely those at the top were given mythical earthly existences. This often resulted in the creation of a variety of contenders for posts. Equally – but this in fact applied only to City Gods – they could be demoted and deprived of their posts. A City God was responsible for the well being of its inhabitants. If there was no rain it was stood in the sun to sweat. If this didn't work it could be whipped and informed that the God was "not divine on his own account, it was his worshippers that made him so".

But not all Gods are involved in this bureaucracy. Many Gods operate a Personal Ministry. These Gods are the most popular and their rise is punctuated by Imperial Edicts giving them titles: Duke, Lord, King, Emperor, Princess, Queen. They do not belong to the bureaucracy but to the aristocracy.

Much has been made of the fact that Gods are created by Imperial Edict. This is not true. The emperor did sometimes issue Edicts but these were acts of recognition. If an emperor participated in a ceremony this also was taken as official recognition but the Gods were created by the people. Many of the Gods probably never received official recognition, being too local to warrant attention. The magistrate who whipped the City God spoke the truth. Gods are not divine on their own account, nor on account of Imperial recognition. They are divine because their worshippers have made them so.

Ancestor Worship

Buddhism — the "other" religion of the Chinese — while having a great effect on China did not in any basic way change the pattern of beliefs. It could only dig itself in by itself changing. Its reverberations were mainly felt in the area of theology but the fact that after two thousand years of influence, a highly educated and intelligent man could still "explain" Chinese religion to me by saying "At the top there is Sakyamuni, the Buddha, and below him there is Kuan Yin and The Jade Emperor" (a Taoist conception) shows that success has been only partial. Buddhism forced Taoism, the religion, to change at the level of dogma but to the peasant in the field there could only be one religion and all manifestations of religion were incorporated into a single conceptual area. This was less true of the more highly educated urban Chinese in the last few centuries who, separated from the land — the source of the abiding religion of the Chinese people — could more easily accept the idea of conflicting and alternative religions. So much so that there are many Chinese Catholics who believe they worship (and therefore do?) a different God than the Protestants (and vice versa). This belief is based on the fact that names given to the Christian God by the two sects are different. The Chinese Catholics worship T'ien Chu, Master of Heaven, and the Protestants worship Shang Ti, the ancient Chinese Supreme God.

It is wrong to say that the Chinese are either Buddhist or Taoist. They are both. A friend told me the following story. When she was young her family rented two rooms from an elderly woman. Every Sunday this woman would disappear to the New Territories. One day she asked the woman where she went. The woman told her of the religious group to whose ceremonies she went. They worshipped five Gods — Lao Tzu, Buddha, Confucius, Allah and Christ!

I say Chinese are both Buddhist and Taoist but one could also say they are neither for, as I hope is already apparent, the springs of Chinese religion are much older than these later accretions.

One of these springs is Ancestor Worship, that untheologized religion which is fundamental to whatever intellectualized beliefs the Chinese profess.

Funeral services at the time of the Shang dynasty were lavish and involved the interment of horses, carriages, vessels as well as of wives. The more important the person, the more people were buried along with him. This was done on the grounds that he would need them in the other world. Also he had to be kept happy for his powers to inflict punishments or grant favours greatly increased after death.

If we compare this with the present day burning of "hell money", paper houses, cars etc., there is little basic difference. The dead exist and have to be accorded their due.

The world of the dead was under the earth — not too far away — in a land called the Yellow Springs from which the water burst forth in Spring. It was a dark female place associated with the North and with Winter. Even at this time the dead retained their hierarchical place in the world of the dead.

In each person there coexists a number of souls. These were divided into two categories; the male and the female. The *Yin* souls were called *P'o* during life and *Kuei* after death. On these souls depended the animal functions. The male souls were called *Hun* during life and *Shen* after death. These were the higher souls. They were related to breath and to the person's name. On death each soul departed. The *Kuei* tended to hang around the corpse for a long time and could therefore be dangerous. Herein lies the source of the belief in ghosts, also of great antiquity.

How this idea of souls melts into the idea that all spirits of the dead eventually revert to the status of *Kuei* in the afterlife (with the exception of the founder of the family) I don't know. The spirits of the common people were worshipped as *Kuei*, while nobles were worshipped as *Shen* for two generations and then became *Kuei*.

There is a story of a ghost that was terrorizing a town; the prime minister of the state made "certain arrangements" which proved effective. Someone asked how these arrangements had worked and the minister replied "when a ghost (*Kuei*) has a place to go to (*Kuei* — a different character) it does not became an evil spirit."

Today, ancestor worship takes a variety of forms. In some households there is a scroll with the names of the ancestors on it. This is often placed in the West hall (the hall of Autumn) and the period of worship covers the first half of the seventh month.

There are also the visits to the graveyard at the festival of Ch'ing Ming in spring and that of Chung Yeung in the late autumn. It is at the former that the bones are cleaned seven or ten years after burial. Both visits involve a meal sharing with the ancestors and traditionally the pork was divided up between the male heirs.

In country areas where a family has grown and become influential over the years this will be expressed by the building of an ancestral hall. Along the end wall of these halls there are plaques on which are written the names of the ancestors.

This use of plaques relates ancestor worship to the Earth Gods and to Confucius who are similarly represented. The Jade Emperor; too, is normally represented in plaque form as is the most recent state cult found in Taiwan, the cult of the Revolutionary Martyrs. The martyrs are those of the 1911 revolution and their descendants, the Nationalist Movement.

The shrines of this cult are, in layout, similar to the Confucius temples. The plaque in the centre reads "Peasants Revolution War Heroes' Shrine Tablet." Dr. Sun Yat Sen is the prime "martyr". Around the walls of the Taipei shrine are details of the martyrs (first rank) and heroes (second rank). One general achieved the status of martyr by refusing to surrender to the communists. Instead he took his own life, insisting that he be preceded in this step by five hundred of his subordinates. This cult may be seen as the ancestral cult of an idea.

Piety on the part of male descendants is the human end of the contract entailed in ancestor worship. It starts with early manhood. Awe attached to the father, the son was expected to carry out his father's wishes. Embedded in this relationship was a barely conscious sense of threat for the father's position would eventually be taken over by the son. This expressed itself in certain prohibitions: the son could not wear his father's clothes or, in large houses, use the same flight of stairs. These prohibitions are long dead but the idea of sexual competition between father and son seems to have had a long life. It was said that a father would often attempt to violate his son's betrothed and if he succeeded the son would be deposed as heir. Nevertheless respect rather than the sense of threat predominated and this attached itself to the mother as much as to the father. This is nicely illustrated by the story of a man who in middle age was scolded and beaten by his mother. He burst out crying because she was too weak to beat him properly.

Ancestors were worshipped long before the Gods were born. This worship comes from a time beyond the reach of historians; a time when nature inspired man to worship trees and rocks, springs and hills. It has endured. The dead continue to look after the welfare of the living just as the living continue to take care of the dead. The power of the father's grave and the strength of the feelings felt for this place were tragically illustrated by a story reported a few years ago in the South China Morning Post. A 24-year-old policeman having lost a large sum of money through gambling went to his father's grave and shot himself dead. His sister, worried by his disappearance went to the grave to ask for her father's assistance. There she found his body.

The dead can provide help but they can also create problems. If the living experience bad luck or worse it may be because they have neglected their duties to their ancestors. A young boy who died some years before may now desire a wife to keep him company in the world of the spirits. A spirit marriage is arranged with a family whose daughter has similarly died unmarried.

Inevitably there are the myriads of dead who have no living family to take care of their needs and provide them with their portion on feast days. They are the Hungry Ghosts. On the seventh month they are let out of Hell to gather what scraps they can. At this time the entire community makes offerings of food and money in order to ward off the potential danger these ghosts pose.

Where do the dead reside? In Heaven? In Hell? In the Yellow Springs? In the air? In the rivers? In the earth? It depends on their status and on the believer. There is no single answer. They are everywhere.

But it is now time to let the Gods themselves take over the story. Some of the most common titles given to these deities are: *Shen* (spirit), *Hsien* (fairy, immortal), *Sheng* (sage, holy one), *Kung* (lord), *Kuan* (ruler), *Hsing* (star) and *Ti* (emperor).

Part Two:
The Gods

Kuan Ti: God of War

In almost every house there is an altar on the wall containing a picture of Kuan Ti, the red-faced God of War. It always faces the entrance for demons and evil spirits do not dare to enter into his presence. There is a story that once, in a provincial town, a troupe of itinerant actors were invited to give a performance at a large mansion some distance from the town. They were told to put on any performance they wished but on no account should it figure General Kuan. When they arrived at the house the lights were on and a large banquet was in progress. People were milling around the gardens and all were enjoying themselves. The players began to entertain the guests who seemed to be very appreciative. However, as time went on, the actors grew more and more annoyed for they were offered no refreshments. Considering this a slight, the actors put on a piece featuring General Kuan. At the sight of him there was a sudden gasp and everything disappeared. The actors found themselves alone in the grounds of a deserted mansion already overgrown with weeds. Only then did the actors realize that they had been hired to entertain an assembly of ghosts.

The role of Kuan Ti is not an easy one for an actor. It is unique in that it demands conformance to strict ritual. For ten days before performing the actor must abstain from meat and sex. Before going on stage he must burn incense before a paper image which is then tucked into the head-dress. Once made up the actor must not chat or joke. After the performance the actor must again bow to the image before burning it and immediately wash his face. Only when he has removed the costume can he relax. This ritual is necessary for several reasons. Kuan Ti is not only a God but he is the greatest and most powerful God in the pantheon. When an actor is made up to look like Kuan Ti, he partakes of the same essence as Kuan Ti. The ritual abstentions are made to purify the body to make it a suitable "locus" for the spirit of the God. It is a time of spiritual danger for the actor. The very first man to have been entered by the spirit of the God was the man who had caused him to be beheaded. That man did not survive the visitation. Kuan Ti was, prior to his deification, a historical figure who lived from 162 AD to 220 AD. He was a mighty warrior of great repute and his story is told in one of the earliest Chinese novels *The Romance of the Three Kingdoms*.To understand his contribution to the following events it is necessary to sketch in the main outlines of the period.

The virtue of the Han dynasty, set up by a peasant rebel in 202 BC, had begun to run out. The young Emperor Han Huan was completely dominated by eunuchs whose insatiable greed placed heavy burdens on the people in the form of taxes. When society is off-balance the heavens reflect this. Natural disasters seemed to occur with unnatural frequency. There were earthquakes, plagues of locusts, floods and droughts. In response to these the people turned to health cults, and other religious movements. The people began to organize. In 184 AD the strongest of these movements launched a rebellion. They called themselves the Yellow Turbans after the scarves they tied round their heads. This rebellion posed a major military threat to the emperor who divided his army in two, one under the control of the eunuchs, the other under the military. These two factions clashed and the eunuchs lost. In revenge for the murder of the military commander-in-chief 2,000 eunuchs lost their heads. This occurred in 189 AD. When the reigning emperor died without a direct heir a new emperor was found but from now on he was to be a mere tool for a succession of warlords, the last of whom was Ts'ao Ts'ao.

Ts'ao Ts'ao was the most efficient and ruthless of them all. In one year he rose from being a minister without a base or an army to a general with both. He did this by raising a contingent of 5,000 men and when he heard that Yen Chou in Northern China was being beseiged by Yellow Turbans he offered to rid the district of this scourge if they made him their "protector". They agreed and Ts'ao Ts'ao undertook such a successful campaign that 300,000 Yellow Turbans surrendered to him. He organized them into a disciplined army and was now a power to be reckoned with. His most famous words were "I would rather betray the whole world than let the world betray me".

The next thirty years was a time of chaos, of shifting allegiances and of military entrepreneurialship until gradually the situation resolved itself with a temporary division of the country into 3 kingdoms, each headed by a self-styled emperor. The three kingdoms were Wei, in the north, Wu, in the south and Shu in the west. This then is the background to the story of Kuan Ti.

The story starts in 184 AD when prefects and governors throughout China called for volunteers to fight against the Yellow Turbans. Three men met by accident and, discovering they were united by a common purpose, they decided there and then to enter the bond of blood brotherhood and pledge themselves to each other. They took the oath in a peach orchard and sacrificed a black ox and a white horse to sanctify the occasion. The three men were Liu Pei, Chang Fei and Kuan Yu.

Liu Pei claimed to be an impoverished scion of the imperial family. His brothers accepted this claim and he was made the "elder" brother. Presented as a man of honour, he nevertheless comes across as a weak man who was intelligent enough to recognize the fact. Perhaps his was the still centre of the archetypal Taoist ruler as he attracted and maintained the services of many able people.

Chang Fei, the "younger" brother was a butcher and wine-seller by trade. A man of immense appetite, impetuosity and extravagant emotion, he is the embodiment of the fiery, unyielding upholder of justice.

Kuan Yu is an altogether more austere and powerful figure. From the very first moment he commands respect. He is the personification of integrity. Nevertheless he remains enigmatic.

When these three meet, Kuan Yu had been an outlaw for several years. One version of this story which also explains the red face goes like this:

One day while passing the house of a neighbour he heard the sound of weeping. He stopped to enquire the reason. Inside the house was an old man and his beautiful daughter. The old man told Kuan Yu, whose name at that time was Yun-chang, that the uncle of the local official wished to take his daughter as a concubine even though she was already engaged to be married. The official was intent on obtaining the girl for him. Yun-chang flew into a rage, seized a sword and rushed off to kill both the official and his uncle. He now had to flee and the only way out was through the T'ung Kuan mountain pass. As he was wondering how he would be able to get through without being recognized he stopped to wash his face in a mountain stream. There he caught sight of his face which had turned red. He presented himself to the officers at the pass knowing they would not recognize him, told them his name was Kuan, and got through. This story is actually based on an extended pun for "Kuan," same tone, can mean: "to observe", "distressed", "infirm", "widower", "official", "coffin" and "run a thread through the web"; and when he presents himself at the customs post and calls himself "Kuan", a common enough surname, the same character also means "to shut a door", "a mountain pass" and "a time of danger".

The three brothers recruited and equipped 300 men and joined the wars where they made a small name for themselves. When the initial impetus of the uprising collapsed they retired with some small rewards.

It was not until some years later that Kuan Yu first came to wider notice. The occasion was a battle between the warlord Tung Cho, whose puppet the emperor was, and the army of "loyalists" under general Yuan Shao. Liu Pei was accorded the honour of sitting at the general's table and his brothers stood in attendance. The champion from the opposing army was hurling challenges to combat and two captains were sent one after the other to deal with him. Both were killed. Yuan Shao called for someone to take up the challenge but was taken aback when Kuan Yu said he would go. The contest of champions, like the European tradition of chivalry, was a contest of knights. It was an aristocratic affair. It was not for upstart "archers". Nevertheless Kuan Yu insisted and when offered a stirrup cup (by Ts'ao Ts'ao) he told him to pour out the hot wine as he would be back soon. The wine was still warm when he deposited his opponent's head at the general's feet. Yuan Shao was not mollified but Ts'ao Ts'ao was impressed.

As the battle lines wavered and changed and alliances constantly shifted, Liu Pei and his brothers went from one patron to another; to all except Ts'ao Ts'ao. Kuan Yu proved himself at arms time and again with his sword "black dragon" and his horse "red hare" and it was his ability that Ts'ao Ts'ao wanted. Hoping to seduce Kuan Yu to his side he developed a ruse which worked and Kuan found himself trapped half-way up a hillside. Knowing that he was quite prepared to die — "Death is only a return home" was his only comment on the prospect — a friend was sent to talk him over. He finally agreed to submit but only on three conditions: the most important of which was that he be allowed to rejoin Liu Pei if he heard news that he was still alive — this being in doubt at the time. The conditions were accepted but only because Ts'ao hoped to compromise him into staying with him. He attempted to compromise him in a hundred small ways. First he allocated Kuan Yu the same quarters as Liu Pei's wife and concubines who had also been captured but Kuan deflected this stratagem by standing outside their door the whole night holding a candle. Then Ts'ao bestowed on

Kuan the rank of General, presented him with ten lovely serving girls and loaded him with presents of gold and silk. Finally he attempted to compromise him militarily by having him fight as a champion against the army of Liu Pei's patron. All to no avail. When news of Liu Pei did arrive Kuan Yu left everything he had been given and taking his sisters-in-law and his own body of personal guards forced his way through six mountain passes. Throughout this entire episode he showed such a fine appreciation of his duties that even Ts'ao Ts'ao could not feel he had been deserted.

It was this that set him apart from the other heros of the time. His military prowess, great though it was, was often equalled. One champion fought both him and Chang Fei together without retreating. He is not worshipped for his might but because he is the embodiment of "right action", of integrity and of loyalty. He was set a stiff test and he came through without a blot on his reputation. This, at least, is the theory but one should add that his awesome reputation as a warrior is not a negligible element in the equation. It is really the fusion of "might" and "right" that led to his deification. Some say he is worshipped because he is the embodiment of the sacred principles of the *hsieh*, or knight. There is an element of this but chivalry in China had rather different principles to that of Europe.

The European chivalric tradition was bound up with tests of strength in jousts and tournaments, with romantic notions of illicit love and was wholly aristocratic in its perspectives, that is to say arrogant and ignorant. Battles were fought in a manner that went against good sense simply to conform with ideology. If it looked as though the pike men and archers were likely to win without a cavalry charge, the knights would nevertheless charge and trample down their own army because a battle had to end with knights covered in glory. Glory is a very curious concept and quite absent from Chinese notions of chivalry. In China any man could rise to be a knight if he was able to afford or steal (?) a horse and weapons and if he had the necessary prowess. There were no romantic illusions concerning women and the idea of proving oneself for a woman was wholly foreign. Lastly, and most importantly, the Chinese knight did not feel that a personal test of strength had priority over victory. Stories of champions feigning retreat, or defeat, to lure an enemy into a trap litter the pages of the *Romance of the Three Kingdoms*. The knight was given his instructions by a strategist who could be, and usually was, low-born. Kuan Yu, "brother" of Liu Pei though he was, scrupulously obeyed the orders of Liu Pei's Commander-in-chief, Chuko Liang, whose position did not depend on family connections but simply on his brilliance.

Chuko Liang, or Kung Ming to give him his more familiar names, at the age of 26 had acquired, without apparently doing anything, a reputation as a man of great wisdom. Liu Pei visited his cottage three times unsuccessfully in order to meet him and ignored Chang Fei's impetuous suggestion that they should simply send soldiers to drag him out. Kung Ming eventually agreed to help Liu Pei in his struggle and so effective was he that the strategist who opposed him, Chou Yu, died of frustrated impotence at the age of 36. His last words were "Oh God, since thou madest me, why didst thou also create Liang?"

By ruthless strategy Kung Ming pitted the men of Wu against the men of Wei and took the spoils of victory, Chingchou, as the territorial base for Liu Pei. He then appeased the aggrieved victor by saying that they had only borrowed this territory temporarily and would return it. From this base Liu Pei was invited into Szechuan, took that over and so, in effect, divided the country into three competing kingdoms.

Kung Ming seems to have also been something of a Shaman for he is often described as wearing a "Taoist" cloak and conducting sacrifices. He was wearing such a cloak when, caught in a small town with only a handful of troops by a large force of the enemy, he opened the town gates and sat on the wall. Recognizing him they immediately feared a trap and departed without offering combat.

It is interesting to note in the novel that as Kung Ming gains prominence Kuan Yu begin to drop out of sight. When the main army moved to Szechuan he remained in Chingchou. Something has been glossed over. It is only when events move inexorably towards his death that he once again takes the centre of the stage. Was there jealousy or an estrangement? Was it that he was showing too much arrogance or independence to be useful to Kung Ming?

We are left to guess. It is more than likely that the intransigence of age was beginning to show. When Liu Pei was persuaded to style himself emperor in 219 AD, Kuan Yu was not present though he was accorded high honours. Another hint that he was encouraged to lead a sedentary life lies in the fact that Liu Pei found him a wife by whom he had a son and a daughter. When asked to ally his family with that of the Sun's of Wu by giving his daughter in marriage, Kuan flared, "How can my tiger daughter marry with a dog's whelp?" This arrogant answer ultimately led to his downfall but not before he proved that at the age of 58 he had lost little of his spirit. Wounded by a poisoned arrow he allowed his arm to be cut open and scratched to the bone by a doctor while he played a game of chess, showing no sign of pain. Invited to dinner and knowing an ambush had been laid he nevertheless went alone and so petrified his host that the signal to attack was never given. However, he relied too much on his right arm and did not give enough thought to strategy. He was outwitted, captured and beheaded.

On the night that he died his spirit appeared to a venerable Buddhist priest who gave him brief instruction in the law. Kuan became the guardian spirit of that place. So ends his story according to the *Romance of the Three Kingdoms* which was written in 1394 or thereabouts.

His posthumous career however developed and by the seventh century his cult was sufficiently strong to be adopted by the Buddhists. In 1102 the Sung emperor, influenced by his Taoist advisors received him into the official religion as Duke. In 1128 he became Prince and in 1594 he was promoted to Emperor and given the titles "Great Emperor who Seconds Heaven", "Great Emperor who Protects the State" and "King of Military Pacification". He was further raised in 1813 to "Military Emperor" as he is personally supposed to have prevented the assassination of the emperor. At this time it was decreed that he was to be accorded honours equal to Confucius. They do seem to complement each other. Confucius is patron of internal harmony and Kuan Ti, Emperor Kuan, is patron of the security of the frontiers from external threat. Remarkably apt given his surname. It appears that temples, similar to those of Confucius, were built in all administrative districts of the empire and it was in these temples that the executioner's sword was kept. After an execution the magistrate would pray there "for fear the ghost of the criminal might follow him home." No malevolent spirit would dare enter Kuan Ti's presence.

Kuan Ti's way with demons and malefactors makes up in effectiveness what it loses in subtlety. This is amply illustrated by the following story:

A rich man died young. While the family was still mourning him a magician arrived who said that he could bring the man back to life but would need a substitute who would be willing to die in his place. None of his wives appear to have been interested but an old servant did agree so preparations were made. The old man prayed to Kuan Ti explaining his action and then the ceremony began. Suddenly there was a great clap of thunder and the magician was struck dead by lightning. When his body was inspected it was found to have the following burnt on his skin "Condemned by Heaven as a corrupter of religion, a destroyer of the law, who by changing bodies aimed at wealth is executed forth with in accordance with orders received." The magician had meant to send his own spirit into the body.

This mention of "orders received" is rather cryptic but may refer to the fact that the deed had not been done personally by Kuan Ti but by one of his assistants who are normally referred to as assessors. All trades, guilds or occupations have a patron God. Kuan Ti, or Kuan Kung, as he is often known, is patron not only of the military, and of the Ching Emperors but also of restaurants, pawn shops, curio dealers, of certain aspects of wealth and, curiously, of literature. He is said, in this context, to have been able to memorize an entire book at one reading. This last patronage is indeed strange and may be a sign that he was moving in on Confucius' territory, he being patron of bureaucrats and scholars. Kuan Kung is also tutelary guardian of all brotherhoods, secret societies such as Triad organizations, evidenced by his popularity among emigre Chinese communities, and in Hong Kong of the police force, especially the C.I.D. Every C.I.D. office is graced with a large altar to Kuan Kung. It is a nice touch to have the triads and police praying to the same patron.

Kuan Ti's major festivals fall on the 15th day of the second moon and on the thirteenth day of the fifth moon; that is to say, in the centre of the central halls of Spring and Summer (see magic square). Green is the colour of spring and red, that of summer. Summer is the season whose direction is South. South is the direction of life. The front door of a house is considered to face in this direction whether it does or not. Kuan Kung presides over the South; he is protector of the living and of the doors. If we look at his image we see that he is seated on a tiger skin, sometimes he had a tiger's face emblazoned on his chest. The tiger is the animal emblem of the West and of Autumn. Kuan Ti, thus presides over the light half of the year.

Chang Fei, whose wide eyes stare out of a black face and whose bristling beard seems to add to the bristling ferocity of his expression clearly represents the dark end of the year. If their two characters are anything to go by, Summer would appear to be a time of austerity and Winter a time of drunkenness and wild emotion. Chang Fei is said to have been murdered by his own subordinates while deep in a drunken stupor.

Liu Pei, the third of the trio, the one whose characteristics are most humane and moderate, is the embodiment of the Imperial ideal and thus has his place in the centre. It is he who is carrying the seal of

Heaven's authority though he seems to be doing so on behalf of Kuan Kung.

Out of the history of an emperor designate we have a myth of the ideal ruler guarded by the forces of summer and to a lesser extent that of winter.

The story of Kuan Yu and his rise to Kuan Ti is the most illustrious example of an historical man's deification. This was one source of Gods, but by no means the only one.

I have called Kuan Ti "God of War". This is how he is commonly referred to by English writers on Chinese mythology. It is not a very accurate label. He is no bellicose war-mongering god. If anything his lable should be "God who defends the state, civilization and morality".

Pak Tai:
Emperor of the North

When a friend of mine was enquiring about Pak Tai, a young acquaintance of his told him quite confidently that Pak Tai was none
other than Kuan Ti in another guise. He was wrong but there is a reason
for his error. They do much the same job in Heaven. They are both
military protectors of the state and many of the associations of one
have been ascribed to the other. Of the two, Pak Tai's origins are, by
far, the older so it would seem that this passage of associations has
largely been one way.

In order to fit him into the Taoist scheme whereby Gods achieve
their place in the Heavens through a prior earthly existence several
biographies have been mooted.

One account says that he lived around 2,000 BC and was responsible for introducing flood control and drainage systems. Another has
it that he was a sage who practised perfection on the mountain Wu
T'ang Shan. Because of his attainments he was invited by one of the
immortals to join their company. Yet another says that his family
name was Li — the same as Lao Tzu's — and that he lived in the Chou
dynasty. One day while washing his feet in a stream on Wu T'ang Shan
he was called to Heaven to aid them in defeating two monsters who
were ravaging the northern districts. It is also said that he was an orphan
who was brought up by an aunt. He had an aversion to water but one
day he demanded a bath. When he had washed himself he told his aunt
not to throw the water away. This insistence seemed nonsensical and
she ignored it. Next morning she heard a lot of noise in the street
outside her house and went to investigate. Her neighbours were busy
collecting gold from the gutter and she herself only managed to pick up
a few nuggets. She ran up to her nephew's room but he had already
been transferred to paradise. Only then did she understand the meaning
of his order — he had foreseen his death.

There are many other variations built round much the same elements: water, barefeet, and sudden transference to Heaven. The manner of his ascent to Heaven is of less important than what he did there. On this point there is much less divergence. Two monsters, a tortoise and a snake, were ravaging the earth. Pak Tai was placed at the head of the heavenly armies and sent to earth to subdue them. Barefoot, his hair flowing over his shoulders and dressed in a long, black robe, Pak Tai engaged the monsters in battle and utterly destroyed them. He then flung them down a huge chasm which exists in Szechuan and which is considered to be the maw of hell. On his return Pak Tai was made First Lord of Heaven.

This event is usually placed at the time of the war of the Chou and Shang dynasties. Another version of the entire story which is current in Taiwan goes like this:

There was once a pig butcher who came to see that his work was evil and wishing to repent, became a hermit. He meditated for a long time but this was not enough to atone for the guilt of killing so many animals. He therefore disembowelled himself and cast his innards into the sea. By doing so he had separated the two souls of his body. His *Shen* rose to Heaven and became a God while his *Kuei* rose out of the sea in the form of two demons – a turtle and a snake. When he saw that they were harming mankind he returned and subdued them. He then placed them in Heaven as the stars of Ursa Major, the northern measure, under his control. He himself controlled them from his palace in the North Star i.e. the Pole Star.

Because the Pole Star is North Star, one scholar in the Ch'ing dynasty put forward the idea that China was not the "Middle" but the "Northern" Kingdom; a heresy that seems to have gone unpunished.

The placing of Pak Tai, emperor of the North, in the North Star clearly associates him with the highest of all the Gods, Shang Ti, Superior Emperor. Shang Ti has no characteristics. Descriptions of him do not exist. He is the unifying principle of the void. He is the absolute. He is the unknowable first cause of the universe. His operations can be subdivided into two aspects. The Dark Heavens and the Moving Heavens. Pak Tai's title is Hsuan T'ien Shang Ti, Dark Heavens, Superior Ruler, and, as we have seen in the introduction, the Yellow Emperor, Huang Ti, is also Moving Heavens' Superior Ruler. Of these two the Moving Heavens are more knowable.

We find an exact parallel here with the philosophical premise in the *Tao Te Ching*. Behind, above and prior to all things is the unnameable, which, if it can be said to be anything, is the harmony of all opposites. This unknowable principle has two more knowable facets: Tao and Te. Both of these are forms of power. Tao is the power behind all manifestations; Te is particularized power. Tao is related to inaction, Te to action. Tao, the "darker than any mystery," is the less knowable of the two. For this reason Tao can also refer to the Nameless that is behind Tao and Te. Pak Tai is popularly known in Taiwan as "Shang-Ti Yeh" or Grandfather Superior Ruler.

What are this God's origins? Where is his place in the order of things? When the Chou dynasty broke up into rival fiefdoms one of the most powerful was the domain of Ch'in. It was the Lords of this territory who gave birth to the concept of instituting Gods by proclamation. The Green Emperor (East) was created by Duke Hsuan (675-664 BC); the Yellow and Red Emperors (Centre & South) by Duke Ling (424-415 BC) and the White Emperor (West) by Duke Hsien (384-362). It was their descendants who became the emperors of the Ch'in dynasty. Ch'in Shih Huang Ti, the first emperor of that dynasty chose black as his Imperial colour. Nevertheless black seems also to have been associated with the Han dynasty which superceded the Ch'in. Lacquer ware which began to be produced in these times was originally coloured black, though as lacquer itself is transparent this can only have been symbolic in intent. Liu Pang became Han Kao-tsu on ascending the Imperial throne. Kao-tsu means "Supreme Ancestor". It is he who is credited with instituting the cult of the Black Emperor.

During the Sung Dynasty the need to systematize the universe was felt. They attempted to create an Imperial pantheon. For a God to be incorporated there had to be a manifestation. And so it came to pass that in 1118 AD the Emperor's Shaman invoked Pak Tai to appear. The sky darkened and there was thunder and lightning. Suddenly the emperor and his court saw a great turtle and a huge serpent appear in the sky. In a flash they disappeared to be replaced by a single bare foot standing in the courtyard. Unable to see the entire personification, the emperor begged the God to reduce his size. Pak Tai complied and the emperor saw in front of him a ten-foot tall man, bare-footed and grave-faced. He wore a black robe and carried a sword. There is no record of a conversation.

If we are to comprehend Pak Tai's true stature we must leave behind us this mish-mash of stories and go back to the very beginnings of Chinese civilization, before the advent of towns and lords, cities and kings. We must go back to the earliest conceptions of space.

The earliest division of the world was in sexual terms. There was *Yin*; female, active in winter and dark places, and *Yang*; male, active in summer and in the full light of day. *Yin* was associated with the North, *Yang* with the South. Ideas connected with death posited that the dead lived in a place under the earth called the Yellow Springs. These springs were the source of running water. In winter they dried up, in spring they began to flow again containing the souls of the dead who wanted to return to life. The Yellow Springs were therefore *Yin*, while running water was *Yang*. They were both a prison of the dead and conversely the reservoir of life. But if running water was male, the earth that it renewed had to be female.

Domestic earth was female and it appears that a man went to live with his wife's family and the name that was passed on to the children was that of the wife. When a child was born the first action was to place it on the ground. The dying too were placed on the ground and when they were dead they were buried with the head to the north.

Later, in the feudal period, the practice of mourning was developed into a highly complex system. The first son had to withdraw from life for a period of time. He had to walk barefoot, wear only a loose cloak, sleep on the earth and abstain from all things. He could not wash until his mourning was over.

Similar ideas relating to water are evident among the Mongols though it took a different form. They placed a sacred prohibition on washing in running water.

In the feudal period space was further organized. Spiritual Guardians were placed at the four compass points. Meanings and attributes were distributed amongst the four emperors. The north was assigned earth. Earth = life; north = death.

At this time too the cult of Heaven was established. It was an official cult. Heaven was all seeing and the source of all moral authority. The lord was the Son of Heaven. It was through him that earth and heaven were bound. If there was chaos in Heaven then too there was, inevitably, chaos on Earth. As the heavens were the source of order and of time and the seasons, so his son too ordered time by his actions. He wore black in winter. He inaugurated spring by ploughing a furrow in the field of the Earth God.

Despite this care, or perhaps as a sign that the lord had been lax in the performance of his duties, the Heavens periodically showed their disapproval in the form of a solar eclipse. When this happened all the people of the towns would be drawn up into ranks, each wearing the colour of his division. The lord and his attendants wore yellow and stood in the centre of the square. Society was reconstituted in its ideal form. At the moment of greatest danger arrows were fired at the sun and drums beaten to keep at bay the Celestial Dog who threatened to devour the sun. This association of Heaven and Earth is manifest in the language, *Tien* with a high tone means: Heaven, sky, day and to increase; *T'ien* with a high falling tone means: peaceful, gentle flow of water, fields, to cultivate land and the noise of a drum. To this day pots and pans are beaten throughout an eclipse.

Pak Tai is the overlord of the realms of the dead but, as the Yellow Springs are the source of the springs of life, so too does he partake in generation and fertility. As the ancestors are spiritual guardians of their descendants so also is Pak Tai Guardian of Society and thus First General of Heaven's Armies. As wealth depends on fertility, gold is related to running water.

I was told this story: A man who had had a run of bad luck rented a shop which stood at a bend at the bottom of a hill. Facing a road seemed inauspicious. Whenever it rained, however, the water rushed down the road and swirled into his premises. The annoyance of having to mop it up was adequately compensated for by the sudden improvement in his luck. The business flourished and in many other ways fortune smiled.

When chaos reigns and there is destruction Pak Tai is believed to descend from Heaven to restore peace and order. Here he is identified with the very principle of regularity which underlies all things and which is Shang Ti's province.

On the Island of Cheung Chau he is revered as a life-giver for it was his agency that brought to an end a plague that hit the island at the end of the last century. His temple is called the Palace of Jade Vacuity. The idea of "Jade Vacuity" or "Void" is a clear identification with Shang Ti.

Before Pak Tai became personified the North was ruled over by the "Dark Warrior", the Tortoise. The tortoise was seen not only as supporting the Heavens but as representing them. Its shell symbolized the vault of the sky and its belly the earth which moves upon the water. The tortoise is a creature with hybrid characteristics. It is amphibian, an animal of the land and the water. It goes underground in the late autumn and re-emerges in spring. It thus follows the water. In winter it dwells in the "Yellow Springs" and in spring when the waters gush forth it too re-emerges. The absence of visible sexual organs makes it an ideal embodiment of *Yin* the female principle that dominates the dark season. It is considered to be an unchaste animal and "son of a tortoise" is a colloquial term for "bastard". Conversely it is thought to be able to conceive by thought alone. It is interesting that the idea of fertility seems necessary – no doubt an inevitable extension of the idea that the world of the dead is the source of new life. The last expression of this idea is the inclusion of a snake – image of the male principle, son of the dragon of spring – itself a hibernating reptile. We remember that Huang-ti and Nu Kua were half-snake and half-human. Together these two animals symbolize the ambiguous potency of the winter season.

Because the tortoise visits the world of the dead who are the source of regeneration and who as spirits have access to the knowledge of the future, the shell is used for divination.

In early times the tortoise was sacrificed and a question was asked. The shell was then passed through the sacrificial fire and the cracks on the surface gave either a "Yes" or "No" answer. Later, when the system of trigrams was invented, its source was attributed to the markings on the tortoise shell. To this day fortune-tellers will shake three coins in a tortoise shell. *Kuei*, meaning tortoise, is identical in sound to the word for "compasses, rule, law" (規), a tone difference relates it to "a hill spring" (氿), a place of religious significance, and "spirit" (鬼). Is it because the tortoise shell sounds like "law" that it became of divinatory significance or did its divinatory significance suggest the idea of law? It is a tantalizing but unanswerable question.

We have come a long way from the story of the orphan whose bathwater turned into gold, yet there still remains the mystery of the warrior image. Is this because he is the executioner (*Kuei*) who kills enemies and traitors (*Kuei*) to enforce the law (*Kuei*)? Is it because winter was the season of military conflicts – when one lord waged war on his neighbour? War was never called war but punishment – to rectify a trespass against the law.

Lastly let us look at his hand gesture. The arrangement of hands is used in Buddhist art to clarify the symbolic meaning of a particular representation. One of these gestures – or mudra – has the upright index finger of the left hand sheathed by the fist of the right hand. This mudra means the suppression of darkness. This is an apt – almost humorous – touch for Pak Tai is the Lord of Darkness and so his index finger remains unsheathed.

The Purple Planet

There is something rather disturbing about this God. He is not formally attired. He does not look Chinese. He is out of the pattern.

The characters on the plaque are the same as those across the top and can be translated as "The Purple Planet looks straight". It is this ability to look straight, that is, to the heart of things that is represented by the round staring eyes. To see the true nature of a thing is to know that thing and clearly this knowledge is helpful in combat. Sun Tzu, the Chinese military genius, summarized this in a well-known saying "Know your enemy, know yourself, a hundred fights, a hundred victories".

The Purple Planet is in fact the Pole Star which, because of its fixity in the Heavens, had a very special significance — that of imperial stability. His image acts as a defence against evil spirits.

Like all ancient civilizations the Chinese posited a relationship betwen the order of society and the harmony of the Heavens. The Heavens — and the way in which they were ordered became an idealized mirror of earthly concepts. Observation of the stars dates from the very earliest times and this observation, and the naming and ordering of the universe, continued until about the Sung dynasty when it reached its final shape. When the Jesuits came four to five hundred years later interest in the stars had stagnated. The Jesuits provoked a new interest. They were able to do so, in part, because the power of the forces behind the symbols also seems to have stagnated into little more than formal concepts.

The Chinese posited five directions: North, South, East, West and Centre. Each had a colour and animal association.

The Purple Star was the dwelling place of the spirit of the Universe, T'ai Yi, the Great Unity. On either side of the Pole Star are the two Ursa constellations; the big and little dipper. The Chinese refer to these as the Northern and Southern Measures respectively. The measures in question are the measures of rice, life, that each man is allotted. The

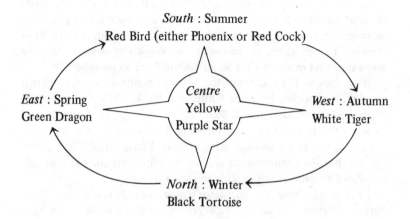

South : Summer
Red Bird (either Phoenix or Red Cock)

East : Spring
Green Dragon

Centre
Yellow
Purple Star

West : Autumn
White Tiger

North : Winter
Black Tortoise

Southern Measure is the seat of the God who records births, the Northern Measure is the seat of the God who records deaths. This northern constellation is also the seat of several other Gods: Tin Hau, Tou Mou — the Goddess of Measure, K'uei Hsing, the God of Literature and also of the highest God in Heaven, Shang Ti. It is strange that Shang Ti — or his later personification, the Jade Emperor, should be seen to reside in Ursa Major. The answer to this is that the tail of Ursa Major swings round the pole (which is a spatial area and not a star. The Pole Star being that which is nearest the centre of this space). By observing it at the same hour every evening one can determine the seasons. When first visible in the evening the end of the tail points north in winter, east in spring, south in summer and west in autumn. Here we have the origin of the directional associations of the magic square. The constellation came to be seen as the Jade Balance by which the Jade Emperor regulated the seasons.

The polar space became known in the early Han dynasty as the Purple Forbidden Enclosure. Stars that would have been used as former pole stars can be found from the names given them. Thus, we have T'ien I, Celestial Unity, and T'ai I, Great Unity which would have been pole stars in the earlier and later part of the second millennium BC. This shows how old Chinese cosmological ideas are. We then have a star named T'ien Shu, Celestial Pivot, which was the Pole Star in Han times. Our Purple Planet was thus a movable one.

As Ursa Major is more dependable than the Pole Star, as it "dictated" the seasons through some potent power, and because it is a great deal more visible, it was a more suitable Residence of the Supreme Ruler of Heaven. The emperor, to encourage an auspicious destiny, had the seven stars that make up Ursa Major embroidered on his robe.

If we look at the colours of the compass points we see that there is a colour opposition between White and Black, allying Autumn and Winter; between Green and Red, allying Spring and Summer, and between Purple and Yellow symbolizing the unity of the Centre by the coalescence of two complementary colours. I have called East's colour "green" but the Chinese word is *ching* which in this context is usually translated as azure but has a wide spread of reference.

"The word *cheng* is a translator's nightmare. It can mean "blue", "green", "azure", "black", "pale yellow" and the white of an egg." (Hugh Baker: *South China Morning Post*, 4 Nov. 1979).

As to the complementarity of Yellow and Purple, we find further reverberations of this idea in the fact that the residence of the emperor (colour yellow) was known as the Purple Palace and again in the fact that scholars who had passed the doctorate exams were presented with a purple gown, clearly emphasizing, along with the high place accorded to K'uei Hsing, God of Literature, the importance to the state of power being complemented, and made whole, by intellect. The Goddess of the lavatory is the "Purple Lady". Our own euphemism for the lavatory, the throne, is perhaps a vestige of a similar idea or evidence of a similar sense of humour. There is another opposition hidden in the diagram: that of sex. The Tiger and the Dragon are male, the Tortoise (because of the absence of visible genitalia) and the Phoenix are female, giving us a *Yin* (female) – *Yang* (male) diagram:

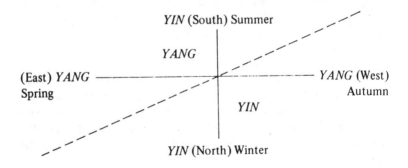

The dotted line shows the division of the year. The Autumn-Winter coalescence is the *YIN* half of the year; the Spring-Summer axis is *YANG*. But herein lies a problem for while the emblem of the North, seat of *Yin*, is female so too is the emblem of the South which is the major seat of the *Yang* powers. It is because of this problem that the nature and sex of the "red bird" is ambiguous. As emblem of *Yang* it becomes a cock.

The origins of these concepts are unknown to us but they show an intent to structure the entire universe in symbolic terms. But as the same structure has to resolve a wide range of relationships, layer upon layer of symbol has been built up which cannot be satisfactorily explained in a two dimensional model. The symbols operate on several planes at the same time. The fullest expression of this is the *Fung-sui* compass which has 24 "rings", or concentric circles, each of which has its own significance. Each ring can be seen as a separate symbolic plane. It is perhaps the most complex structural system ever created. It attempts to be an entirely closed and all embracing system. Such an attempt can only be a magnificent failure in real terms or so facile as to be worthless. The "science" of *fung-sui* belongs to the first category.

Just as society centred on the Lord so did the universe on the Pole. Their unity of function was seen and put to use. Feudal religion centred on the seasons and so gave primacy to that constellation that regulated the seasons, Ursa Major. Shang Ti lives both in the Purple Star and in Ursa Major depending on whether and the imperial or the seasonal idea is being referred to.

Under the Sungs the systemization of the Heavens reached its fullest expression. But the Sungs fell to the Mongols who, in turn, gave way to the Mings. The Imperial Cult ossified. Astronomy as a science deteriorated and was in a sad state when the Jesuits arrived.

Around the year 1600 Matteo Ricci, the first Jesuit to penetrate China, found in Nanking an observatory filled with astronomical instruments, far superior to any in Europe at the time, which were at least 200 years old. They were no longer in use and no-one knew how to use them. Ricci, and the Jesuits who followed, were all schooled in astronomy. They used their knowledge to pry their way into the court and thus gained a limited acceptance. Ricci eventually found himself in the unenviable position of maintainance man-cum-entertainer. He alone knew how to repair the numerous Imperial clocks — gifts from foreign emissaries — and, possessed with a photographic memory, could recite large numbers of characters, written at random on a sheet of paper, having glanced at it for only a few minutes. This was a party trick that enabled him to gain entrance to many a noble's home. He and his successors taught the new astronomy of Europe and as a result of their influence some stars gained new astrological significance. The God of Longevity shifted from Ursa Minor to Libra and the twin stars of Gemini became the seat of *Yin* and *Yang*; something of a comedown for these two forces. These were major changes to the system yet no political repercussions seem to have resulted, suggesting that the Chinese world had changed, the emperor paying only lip service to the idea of cosmic support. Certainly in T'ang times such innovations would have been punished severely. Court Astronomers were encouraged to be secretive about their business as rebels might make use of calendrical calculations. A new system of the universe could only have adverse effects on the present system of society.

It is time to leave the subject of Astrology and Astronomy and return to our bald man riding his green tiger.

As we have seen, the Purple Planet represents the stability of empire and the harmony of society. It is this latter idea, that of balance and order, which predominates. The image invokes these states with an arsenal of symbols and weapons. The most complex of these is the *baht kua*, or eight trigrams.

The eight trigrams are the eight possible arrangements of broken and unbroken lines placed in series of three. The unbroken line is *Yang*, the broken is *Yin*. The classic book of fate, "The Book of Changes", the *I Ching*, is based on the trigrams doubled up making 64 possible arrangements, each of which has a commentary.

At the centre of the *baht kua* is the *Yin-Yang* symbol. *Yang* — the male half — represents Heaven, sun, light, action, penetration and oneness. *Yin* — the complementary female half — represents earth, noon, darkness, quiescence, submission and duality. The emblem of *Yang* is the dragon and that of *Yin* is the tiger — relating their opposition to the East-West (Spring-Autumn) axis which are the times of the equinoxes at which points the forces of *Yin* and *Yang* are in harmony. East and West are in balance, North and South in opposition.

Yin and *Yang* are the two forces that under-lie all nature. All things came into being through their interaction. All things partake of *Yin* and *Yang*. Harmony results from balance. This is the image of that balance.

The animal has been identified as a tiger but it looks more like a pekinese dog. The tiger is the king of terrestrial beasts and it is renowned for an extensive range of qualities: ferocity, courage, dignity, and sternness among others. It is the most feared of all animals and its image is considered to be a most potent demon dispeller. Soldiers used its image, sometimes going so far as to dress in imitation tiger skins, in the hope that this would strike terror in their opponents. Tigers are still to be found in China and a few centuries back were sufficiently numerous to pose a constant threat. We cannot therefore blame scarcity and resort to the imagination for this composite animal we are presented with. Pekinese dogs were however used as models for the lion, which is not indigenous to China.

The pekinese was often called a lion dog and was prized in the Ch'ing dynasty for this likeness. It was thus accorded favoured animal status in the Ch'ing court. The Lamas of Tibet sent "lion-dogs" to the Imperial court as tribute and the high value attached to these creatures may be inferred from the following instructions laid down by the last Empress Dowager, Tz'u Hsi, on how to treat such a dog should it fall ill: "Anoint it was the clarified fat of the leg of a snow leopard." These instructions were presumably laid down for the Imperial keepers of the dogs whose life expectancy must not have been too great as the instructions go on to say: "If it (the lion-dog) dies, remember that man is not immortal and thou too must die."

The gold ribbon flying around the shoulders is a common reference, especially in statues of temple guardians, to high rank and dignity.

The pillar in the background is more obscure in its significance. The orb represents the sun and the pillar maintains it in its place. Unfortunately, while the metaphor of a "Pole" works in English there is no such linguistic connection in Chinese. The North Pole, the Purple Forbidden Enclosure of the Heavens, is that point around which the constellations rotate. Here is the seat of the power that keeps everything in its place. This is the force that maintains the sun in the Heavens.

The Chinese however are not fatalists. They believe the harmony of the Heavens depends on social harmony. If man is the source of disharmony, corrections can be made. Harmony is a reflection of imperial merit. It is the virtue of the emperor that ultimately supports the sun in the sky. The Purple Planet is the embodiment of harmony.

Kuan Yin:
Hearer of Cries

In a kingdom on the borders of Cambodia or Burma or perhaps even India there was once a king named Miao Chung. He and his wife were childless and as he was nearing the age of 50 it was a matter of great concern to him that he leave a heir. Sacrifices and prayers were offered and eventually answered. His wife gave birth in three successive years to girls: Miao Ssu (sometimes "Ch'ing"), Miao Yin and finally Miao Shan. As there was no son the king decided to settle the succession by marrying his daughters to men of ability and the one who proved himself most able would succeed him. The two elder daughters were married off but Miao Shan refused. Her sole ambition was to attain perfection.

Her father's fury at her obduracy only increased when she stated that she would consent to marriage but only to a physician. On being asked why, she replied, "My wish is to heal humanity of all its ills . . . I wish to equalize all classes, putting rich and poor on the same footing, to have a community of goods, without distinction of persons." Eventually, she persuaded him to allow her to retire to the White Sparrow Nunnery. Here she was given the hardest and most menial jobs on the king's orders. However, Gods and animals all conspired to help her. Discovering this, the king ordered the entire nunnery to be burnt. Miao Shan, with Heaven's help, extinguished the fire. Further attempts at execution failed until she committed suicide by strangling herself. Death, she said, was preferable to her father's hatred.

Her soul now descended to Hell which she soon transformed into a Paradise of Joy. A memorial was sent up to Heaven saying "Since it has always been decreed that in justice there must be both a Heaven and a Hell, if you do not send this saint back to earth there will no longer be a Hell but only a Heaven." Returning to life she was transported by the Buddha of the West to the island of P'u T'o (near Ningpo in Chekiang Province) where she spent nine years perfecting herself.

One day while sitting on the island, which was surrounded by a "dragon haunted sea", she saw that the third son of the Dragon King of the Eastern Sea had been caught by a fisherman and was being taken alive to the market. She sent her attendant, a youth named Shen Ts'ai (Virtuous Talent), who had become her disciple, to buy the fish and return it to the sea. In gratitude for this deed the Dragon King sent her a jewel called the "Night Brilliance Pearl". His grand-daughter, Lung Nu (Dragon Maiden), brought the gift and was so entranced by Kuan Yin's virtue that she remained with her.

At this time Kuan Yin's father was struck down by a mortal illness which could only be cured, he was informed, by the hand and the eye of the "never angry one". An embassy was sent to obtain these. Kuan Yin allowed her hand to be cut off and her eye to be gouged out. Reduced to an ointment, these parts immediately effected a cure. The king then discovered that he owed his cure to his daughter who he had thought dead. Full of remorse, he left his kingdom to his chief minister and became a convert to Buddhism.

This story is one of many variations which play on the same essential theme of a virgin disobeying her father, fleeing to a walled enclosure, being killed and then transformed into a Goddess. Collectively they are known as the Miao Shan legends.

The origin of these legends is attributed to a monk named Tao Suan who lived in the seventh century AD. This monk "went insane" and began to have revelations. In one of these he imagined himself surrounded by Gods one of whom was the female form of Bodhisattva who was named Miao Shan and who was the third daughter of a king . . . etc. His revelations were recorded by his disciples and published after his death. It is likely that he only sketched in the basic outline of the story and the rest is a result of gradual accretion. Miao Shan was invented but she was not yet associated with Kuan Yin whose origins we must now trace.

Her real, or should I say historical, origins are Indian. Her progenitor is Avalokitisvara, a male deity born form a beam of light emanating from a beam of Amitabha Buddha. Avalokita is credited with many earthly incarnations and, except for one occasion when he was incarnated as a horse, all were as human males. He is the all compassionate aspect of the Buddha. As a male he came to China in the first century AD and as a male he remained until the seventh century. From the seventh to the twelfth century a process of change occurred, at the end of which Kuan Yin had become female.

No one is really very sure of how this process occurred or why. One theory is that it was mediated by a Tibetan embodiment of compassion, Tara. Tara was born from a tear shed by Avalokita and is immensely popular both in Tibet and in Mongolia. Her popular function is the rescuing of people from dire hardships and miseries. This is, of course, Kuan Yin's major function. Both Tara and Kuan Yin are young, beautiful girls but whereas Kuan Yin is depicted as demure, Tara is impish.

There is an extraordinary similarity but if that was all there was to the connection we would have to consider the association coincidental. However, it only takes a quick look at the history books to see that the period of sex change occurs at the time when the T'ang dynasty was disintegrating and China was overrun by a succession of armies and presumably of peoples — refugees fleeing from campaigns on the fringes of China.

In 751 the Chinese were defeated by the Arabs in Samarkand and retreated. The Kitans began to menace the borders. In 763 the Tibetans sacked Ch'ang An. The Chinese lost their hold on Manchuria and Korea. Mongolia succumbed to the Turks. China began to fall apart. For the next three hundred years the Kitans remained on the sidelines manipulating the internal dissensions. When the Sung dynasty finally established itself and unified China the emperor found it cheaper and more expedient to pay tribute to the Kitans rather than wage war. And so it goes on. The Kins defeated the Kitans and took over the North of China in 1125, and then up to 1368 China was dominated first by the Kins then by the Mongols.

As Tara was popular in Mongolia we can assume that all these successive tribes favoured her cult and that it was through these invasions that the contact was made. But we must also explain the acceptance by the Chinese people of a female form. The contact was made but it is unlikely that the female form was imposed. If it were imposed it is unlikely it would have lasted. Clearly there was in the female form something that was "right".

Now, although Tara "was born" from Avalokita while Kuan Yin "is" Avalokita they are both transformations of the original male deity and how that is explained depends on the locale. What must be noted is that first in Tibet, then in China, a female deity whose function involved compassion was felt to be necessary and was created. Both Tara and Kuan Yin share a function that is not performed by Avalokita: the patronage of human love, conception and of children. These are functions ideally performed by women. I think it is in this that the "rightness" of a female form lies. But why did Kuan Yin take on these functions at all?

Avalokita arrived in China in the first century AD with the first Buddhist Missionaries but did not acquire the name Kuan Yin until the seventh. Hsuan Tsang, the priest whose journey to India is the subject of the novel *Monkey*, by Wu Ch'eng-en, seems to have been a devotee of Avalokita and it was he who introduced the Chinese translation of the Indian name which is normally considered to mean "Hearer of the Sounds" (of the cries of the world). Now, it is extremely unlikely that he did this without forethought. He wished to popularize Buddhism and so he chose a name that would work in a Chinese context. As most of the people at that time would have been illiterate, when they heard the name Yin it would inevitably have conjured up the additional meaning "the Female Principle". Both are expressed by words having exactly the same tones. I do not think we have to look any further for an explanation of the God's sex change.

It is very interesting that Hsuan Tsang should have implicitly involved female associations at much the same time as another monk was having revelations concerning the female form of the Bodhisattva. Something was clearly in the air, though what that was, we don't know. Nevertheless, Kuan Yin was not associated with the Miao Shan legends until another abbot P'u Chan made that connection during the Sung dynasty, probably some time in the twelfth century when the female form had become accepted. But why were they connected? In part there was a need to sinicize Kuan Yin and give her an acceptable mythology, but there was also a need to convert and Buddhists had long seen the value of stories which would beguile an audience.

The cult of Kuan Yin seems to have become immensely popular at just that time when she was going through her sex change. Her popularity went beyond any denominational limits. Her cult was not confined to Buddhists. We are told that she is also a Taoist Goddess but it is difficult to know exactly what this means unless it is simply that her image became a common sight in non-Buddhist temples. It is an incorrect assumption to say that all that is not Buddhist is Taoist. Most temples exist independently of any overt theology. They are dedicated to a God or Goddess by a community. If a God becomes universally popular, priests of all denominations have to recognize that fact. It appears that she became accepted to the Taoist clergy in the tenth century but her Buddhist origins could not be ignored. She alone of all Chinese deities is not to be offered wine or meat, the normal offering to a God. To do so would be blasphemous. Yet there is a coda to this. Her compassion is so great that should such offerings be made in ignorance they are to be accepted.

The idea that a sin committed in ignorance is no sin does not conform with the idea that names fit things. If one does X, and X is a sin, then, whatever one's intentions, one has committed a sin. Kuan Yin overrides this mechanistic attitude and this gives her a greatness not possessed by other Gods.

Kuan Yin is something quite new in the way of a God. She demands a reverence that no other God can command. Her purity is such that she is often compared to the Virgin Mary, she eclipses even Sakyamuni Buddha. She dispenses her favours liberally without need for recompense. If her name is called in an hour of danger the danger will pass. "Two men − one chanting the names of the 6,200,000 Buddhas, in number like the sands of the Ganges, and the other simply calling on Kuan Yin − have equal merit." Young married couples pray to her for offspring, pregnant women for sons, mothers for the well-being of their children. In this aspect of her being she has assumed the duties of another Goddess − the Princess of the Motley Clouds, daughter of the Great Emperor. This deity can grant the blessing of children and she presides over childbirth. She is accompanied by one attendant who holds an enormous eye and this preserves children from diseases of the eyes. Other attendants are responsible for the major phases of childhood.

Kuan Yin has shown a great ability to assimilate into her own province the responsibilities of other Goddesses. She is able to do this, in Buddhist eyes, by claiming these other Goddesses as manifestations. Tin Hau has escaped this fate but she and Kuan Yin often share the same temple. Kuan Yin has also usurped some of Tin Hau's territory in that she is sometimes called Goddess of the Southern Sea.

Let us now turn to the wealth of symbolism to be found in the glass painting. The halo-ed Kuan Yin is seated on a lotus holding a vase and a willow branch. While Shen Ts'ai is in devoted attendance, the girl Lung Nu stands, holding out the pearl and a bird, half peacock half pheasant, brings her a rosary.

The halo is clearly a visual representation of her enlightenment and need not detain us. Far more complex is the lotus. This plant had a great religious significance throughout all the great civilizations: Egyptian, Greek, Persian, Assyrian, Indian and Chinese. It is the Buddhist symbol par excellence. It symbolises purity, because it grows out of the mud but is not defiled, and perfection because its fruits were said to be ripe the moment the flower blossomed just as Buddha's words of truth bear immediately the fruit of enlightenment. The petals of the flower are seen as the spokes of the wheel of the law of perpetual cycles of existence along which all unenlightened sentient beings are destined to pass. In Avalokita's hands this latter meaning is referred to.

But the lotus had a pre-Buddhist significance in China. It is the emblem of summer and fruitfulness and all its parts related to fertility in some form on account of the number of seeds it contains in its pod. Lotus roots, denoting potency, are one of the gifts traditionally exchanged between a girl and a boy prior to their marriage. Lotus seeds are believed to have aphrodisiac qualities while burnt lotus leaves were considered to be a contraceptive. The whole flower also denotes beauty.

The willow branch is similarly an emblem of beauty; girls were noted for their willow-like waists. This association owed much to the willow's suppleness and seeming frailty which made it the Buddhist symbol of meekness. The willow also has the power of expelling demons and a branch of this tree was traditionally used for sweeping graves. A sprig of the willow worn in the hair was believed to help ward off blindness.

The vase symbolizes harmony and in Kuan Yin's hands is said to contain the Dew of Compassion. Stories are told of her appearing at the bed-side of the seriously ill and sprinkling a few drops of this nectar on their heads. This always resulted in miraculous cures.

The bird with the rosary is a curious cross between a pheasant and a peacock. The former symbolizes beauty and good fortune while the latter is the symbol of beauty and high rank. This latter symbol seems curious until we realize that the "eyes" on the peacocks feathers are really a hidden reference to the Princess of the Motley Clouds and the eye that accompanies her.

Lastly we come to the pearl — the night shining pearl which aids metaphysical vision in the same way as the willow protects its more basic equivalent. The pearl was seen as the concrete essence of the moon distilled through the secret workings of the female principle, *Yin.* Hence it is a charm against fire which is the development of the male principle, *Yang.*

When dragons are depicted they seem to revolve around a red orb which is sometimes described as the sun, the moon, the unity of *Yin* and *Yang* or the night shining pearl. If you look at the roof of a temple there is always an orb in the centre and on each side there are either two carps, symbol of good fortune, or two dragons – the imperial symbol from the Han dynasty onwards. The pearl itself symbolizes perfection.

Kuan Yin's connection with the pearl is echoed again in a story related about the Emperor Wen Tsung of the T'ang dynasty who was addicted to oysters. Fishermen from the oyster areas were forced to supply him with vast quantities for no payment. Now the traditional method of fishing for oysters was to weigh the diver down with a large stone so that he sank to the bottom and then a few minutes later his companions would haul him up. The mortality rate was high. The emperor's addiction was causing great hardship. One day an oyster of exceptional size was served to him but despite all efforts it refused to open. It was about to be removed when it suddenly opened of its own accord disclosing a mother of pearl image of Kuan Yin. A Buddhist monk interpreted the event in the following words: "This matter is not devoid of significance. The Pusa Kuan Yin has chosen this means of inclining your majesty's mind to benevolence and of filling your heart with pity for your oppressed people." The emperor thereupon abolished the levy on oysters and issued an edict that her image was to be admitted to every Buddhist temple in the Empire.'

No other God attracts such a variety of symbols and this is a tribute to her importance, an importance bound up with the fact that she embodies the ideal excellence of all that is female. Her image is a wholly Chinese conception. Born from an accident of history, of language and of cultural displacement, Kuan Yin owes little to her Indian original.

Monkey:
Great Sage Equal to Heaven

Why is it that the three Gods whose stories are most fully developed are all Buddhist and have their origins in India? Their stories are all equally fantastic and unrooted in history. No indigenous God can compete on this level. Was it necessary to flesh out the stories to gain popular acceptance? Perhaps, but if they had been necessary in some way the stories need not have been so elaborate. In Kuan Yin's case the Miao Shan legends seem to have come to birth as an illustration of ideal perfection. Miao Shan means "admirable goodness". The story of Monkey had a much slower germination and, as in the case of Na Cha, (subject of the next chapter) its sheer fantasy is essential to his popularity. Neither Monkey nor Na Cha have reasons for being. They do not regulate the seasons nor do they personify ideal attributes. They are functionless. Both are images of rebellion. They have infiltrated their way into the common stock of folklore and into Heaven through the delight men feel when they hear of their respective exploits.

Knowing that order and balance have such primacy in Chinese thought it is perhaps surprising that a God whose main characteristic is rebellion and subversion should be received with affection. But China has two imaginations, one sober and Confucian, the other impish and Taoist. Monkey appeals to the Taoist in men. Monkey's subversion was not a random activity but aimed at those in authority who refused to recognize his abilities. He is thus a perfect vehicle for the people's desire to confound and upset the bureaucracy that ruled over them. He was not a revolutionary. All he demanded was his rightful place in Heaven — at the top.

The most complete version of Monkey's story is to be found in the novel *Monkey* or, as it is also called, *Journey to the West*. This was written towards the end of the sixteenth century partly as a satire on bureaucracy and is based on the real journeyings of the Monk

Hsuan Tsang who is referred to as Tripitaka. I can do no better than give a brief summary.

"There was a rock that since the creation of the world had been worked upon by the pure essences of Heaven and the fine savours of Earth, the vigour of sunshine and the grace of moonlight, till at last it became magically pregnant and one day split open, giving birth to a stone egg about as big as a playing ball. Fructified by the wind it developed into a stone Monkey, complete with every organ and limb." And so Monkey was born.

Monkey joined up with other monkeys, and soon, because of his bravery, he became their king. Life was good and for a few hundred years he was perfectly happy until one day he suddenly had a premonition of death and decided to look for some way in which he could escape from the wheel of existence. He set out to look for an immortal who could give him the knowledge he needed. After ten years he found one and for another twenty years stayed with him, taking as his name in religion "Aware of Vacuity".

Under the immortal's tuition he received enlightenment, learnt the seventy-two transformations which ensure immortality and the magic formula which enabled him to go cloud-soaring. In the end, however, he disgraced himself and was forced to leave.

He returned to his kingdom to find it bedevilled by the Demon of Havoc. For someone of Monkey's newly learnt attainments it was an uneven battle. Plucking hair from his body he threw them at the demon. Each one turned into an armed monkey. It was a matter of a moment to subdue and kill him.

As a result of this battle Monkey realized that he must have a weapon that matched his abilities. This he obtained from the Sea Dragon of the Eastern Sea. It was the iron pillar with which the Milky Way was pounded into existence. It had the magical property of shrinking and expanding to the size required. Monkey mentally ordered it to reduce itself to the size of a pin and tucked it behind his ear. He now demanded that the Dragon King fit him out with suitable clothing which included "cloud-stepping" shoes. Such was his arrogance that the Sea Dragon immediately decided to report his behaviour to the Jade Emperor.

Not long afterwards Monkey was arrested in his sleep and his soul was escorted to the Land of Darkness where Yama, King of Death, lives. This is the normal procedure of death according to Chinese tradition, but Monkey, who considered himself immortal, was naturally rather annoyed. He demanded to see the files and then erased not only his

Kuan Ti: God of War

Pak Tai: Emperor of the North

The Purple Planet

觀音大士

Kuan Yin

Monkey

Na Cha: The Third Prince

Tin Hau: Queen of Heaven

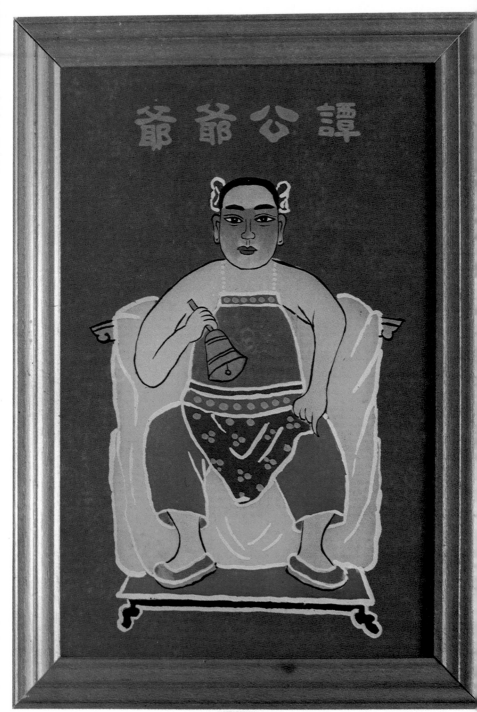

Tam Kung

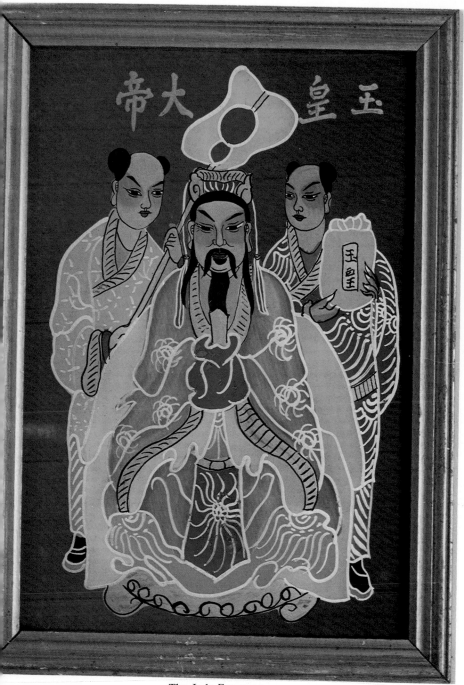

The Jade Emperor

Magistrate Pao

桃花仙女

Peach Blossom Girl

Chang Hsien

Wong Tai Sin

Tsai Shen: God of Wealth

Tsai Shen: God of Wealth

Mother of The Three Islands

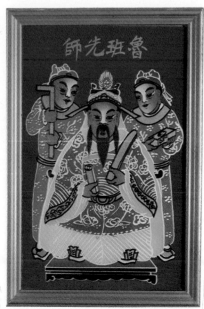

Lu Pan

Lei Kung

Hung Sheng

own name but those of all the other monkeys as well. He then forced his way out of Hell – and woke up. The ten judges of the underworld reported the matter to Heaven.

The Jade Emperor, after hearing the two complaints, decided he must take some action. However he was dissuaded from violence and instead invited Monkey to Heaven so that an eye could be kept on him. Unfortunately there were no immediate vacancies in the Heavenly ministries. The only job available was supervisor of the Imperial Stables. Monkey accepted and took on his duties with great gusto. However, it was not long before he found out that far from being one of the highest positions in Heaven he had been given one of the lowest. In a raging temper he returned to Earth and styled himself "Great Sage, Equal of Heaven". Officers sent to arrest him found themselves unequal to the task. Monkey informed them that he would return only on condition that Heaven acknowledged his title.

The Jade Emperor, once again dissuaded from violence, agreed to the conditions on the grounds that the position had no duties attached to it and was unsalaried.

Monkey's second stay in Heaven was more disastrous. Seeing that Monkey's absence of duties was itself a threat, the Ministers petitioned the emperor to give him the post of Guardian of the Imperial Peach Garden. The peaches grown here are the peaches of immortality. Monkey procceeded to feast himself on them.

Shortly afterwards he gate-crashed, in the guise of an immortal, a banquet to be given by the Queen of Western Heaven. Arriving early he ate and drank himself nearly senseless. Realizing he would soon be discovered, he staggered out and went to pay a call on Lao Tzu. Lao Tzu was out but the door to his laboratory was open. Inside Monkey found some gourds filled with the perfect elixir. Multiply fortified with immortality, he at last faced the fact that Heaven would not be too pleasant for him in the near future and again fled back to Earth.

This time there could be no mercy for him. The entire might of Heaven was hurled at him. A titanic struggle ensued. Heaven found it no easy matter but finally a stratagem was employed and Monkey was caught. He was sentenced to death but after several attempts at execution this was found to be impossible. Even Lao Tzu's crucible could not reduce him – its only effect being to make Monkey's eyes go permanently red. Finally the Buddha of Western Paradise was called on. The Buddha mocked Monkey's pretensions, calling him a jumped up Monkey Spirit. They then entered a wager. Buddha promised Monkey the Imperial Throne of Heaven if he could jump off his, the Buddha's, hand. Monkey leapt off and whizzed so fast he became almost invisible until he came to five great pillars. He landed and left his mark, relieving himself at the same time to show his disrespect. He then somersaulted back. The Buddha showed him his hand and there was the mark he made. Caught, he was imprisoned in a rock mountain and left there for 500 years, only to be released at the instigation of Kuan Yin on condition that he accompanied the pilgrim, Tripitaka, whose journey to India and back takes up the rest of the story. To make sure that Monkey didn't get up to any more mischief Kuan Yin fashioned a metal band which she fixed to his head. Tripitaka only had to say a special prayer for Monkey to be convulsed by pain.

Monkey used his magical abilities to help Tripitaka cross the 80 obstacles that lay in their path. The aim of the journey was to obtain the scriptures which would allow the people of China to attain enlightenment. At the end of the journey, they were blessed with Bodhisattvahood as a reward for their vicissitudes.

This story, the source of endless plots for puppet theatres, is normally attributed to Wu Ch'eng-en (c. 1505-1580). But he did not invent the stories which began to become current from the tenth century onwards. He compiled these legends and formed from them a coherent narrative. An interesting aspect of the book is that it provides us with the exact duration of each episode, with the sole exception of the second stay in Heaven. As Tripitaka was a historical person we can work backwards from this and find Monkey's "date of birth". This works out at the third or fourth century BC. This may be just coincidence, but the oldest version of the Ramayana, the Indian Epic Poem – which features among the major characters the Monkey General, Hanuman – was written at about this time.

The stories involving Hanuman seem to be an obvious source of themes and ideas which occur in the Monkey myth. Hanuman helps Rama, a mortal-immortal, in his search for the thing he desires, in this case his wife. He can fly. He can swell and contract. He is mischievous and finally he, like Monkey, is seen as a White Ape.

Stories of the White Ape first appeared in China in the fourth century AD when, for the first time, Chinese monks were returning from India with a thorough grounding in Sanskrit. They brought with them Indian folk-tales. To spread their message they used folk-tales to illustrate meaning and stories based on animals soon became a popular method of instruction. One of these stock creatures was the White Ape. At this time his character was seen in quite a different light. He was a wholly despicable monster whose appetite was insatiable. He was particularly noted for his despicable tendency of taking advantage of women. Somehow over the centuries this facet of his character disappeared to be replaced by a more endearing cheekiness. Another animal seems to have acquired them — the pig. Monkey was not Tripitaka's only follower — there were two others. Sandy, a river dragon transformed into a white horse, who appears singularly characterless and Pigsy who embodies just those characteristics which were once attributed to the White Ape: brutish appetites and unclean desires.

When the White Ape became an accepted deity is not known but like other Gods he was given his place in Heaven. The two stars of Gemini were his abode. Having no functions, he created his own. Because of his inventiveness he is prayed to for solutions to what appear to be insoluble problems. Because of his power over demons and evil spirits, which beings are considered the cause of illness, he is prayed to for cures and a monkey is often, therefore, part of the baggage of itinerant medicine sellers.

Monkey is also one of the symbolic animals which designate the years, ninth in the series of twelve. Someone born in this year will be mischievous, high-spirited, clever, inventive and sociable but he will also be devious, vain and unscrupulous. Exactly the characteristics one would have suggested. This system of naming years after animals only became fixed during the Yuan Dynasty, and almost certainly originated with the Mongol tribes.

Most people have been contented to assume that Monkey was an import from India yet the motif of a monkey has been found on bronze ornaments dating from the early Han Dynasty. What characteristics were then imputed to this animal is not known but it is possible that the "White Ape" was an indigenous creation used by Buddhist mendicants who gradually overlaid the original image with Indian associations. This however is purely guesswork.

In the glass painting we see him with the accoutrements that have pride of place in the story. His pole is the iron bar he was given by the Sea Dragon, he is holding the peach of immortality, he is wearing his "cloud-stepping" shoes and on his head is the metal band which Kuan Yin placed to ensure this obedience. His halo signifies his enlightenment but as silver is less than gold so Monkey's level among the Gods is lower than that of Kuan Yin.

Na Cha:
The Third Prince

Most gods, chased from reference to reference through the chapters of the standard works, gain in identity, flesh is added to the myth by a name here and a date there. With Na Cha quite the opposite happens. He starts off with all the personality one could want and then, as one tries to disentangle him and fix him in place, he starts to dissolve.

His story starts in a small kingdom. Li Ching, the King, had a wife who was pregnant. As she approached labour, she dreamt that a Taoist priest entered her room. She swore at him for being indiscreet but the priest went up to her and pushed an object to her bosom, saying "Woman, receive the child of a unicorn". She immediately told Li Ching, who thought it all most inauspicious. The pains came on and the child was soon born. There was no doubt about it, it was a freak.

Li Ching decided to kill it and taking his sword, he went into the room where he was confronted by a glowing red light. There was a curious smell and on the floor, rolling around, was a ball of flesh. Li Ching cut it open and a baby emerged surrounded by a halo of red light. His face was white, he had a bracelet on his right wrist and he wore a pair of red silk trousers that gave off a dazzling golden light. The bracelet was the object thrust on the mother by the priest and was in fact the horizon of Heaven and earth.

The priest returned in person the next day and he was allowed in to see the child, on whom he bestowed the name Na Cha. He also claimed that the child would become his disciple. "Na Cha" means "here is a loud cry". He is also commonly known as the Third Prince as he was the third son of Li Ching.

At the age of seven, already over six foot tall, he went for a swim. As he splashed around his red trousers caused the sea to boil which in turn shook the foundations of the Sea Dragon King's temple at the bottom of the ocean. An officer was sent to see what was the problem.

He saw Na Cha and tried to seize him. Na Cha killed the officer with his magic bracelet. Ao-ping, the Dragon King's third son came to settle accounts, and according to one version, there was a series of fantastic but inconclusive fights, "forty bouts", between the two princes until eventually Ao-ping was also despatched. According to another he was immediately killed and had his scales torn off.

The Sea Dragon King decided to inform the Jade Emperor of all that had happened, but he was outwitted by Na Cha who was waiting for him at the gate, invisible. As the Dragon King was about to enter the gates of Heaven, he was thrown to the ground and had his scales ripped off. Only when he promised Na Cha that he wouldn't inform the Jade Emperor was his life spared.

When he returned home he informed his brothers, the Sea Dragon Kings of the other seas, and once again decided to inform the Jade Emperor. He also complained to Li Ching, who was furious with his son. Na Cha admitted his fault and then promptly got involved with the Goddess Shih Chi Niang Niang — he killed her attendant by mistake. She attacked and disarmed him and would have killed him if she hadn't been turned into stone by Na Cha's Taoist master.

However, this escapade allowed the Dragon Kings to capture his parents. He was just in time to stop them and, protesting that it was he who was to be blamed and should therefore pay the penalty, he committed suicide.

Na Cha now appeared to his mother in her dreams and insisted that she build him a temple, threatening her with trouble if she didn't. Li Ching refused to let her but eventually she did so, surreptitiously. The temple soon became known as a miracle shrine and when Li Ching discovered the identity of its inhabitant he ordered it to be burnt down.

This act embittered Na Cha. He felt that he had already given back to Li Ching what was his — his flesh — and swore to revenge himself. He obtained a new body from his master made out of lotus stalks. He was also given as weapons a spear and two wind-fire wheels. Now sixteen feet high and well-armed, he met his father in battle. Li Ching was defeated and forced to flee. Undeterred by his elder brother who charged him with unfilial conduct, Na Cha chased after and cornered Li Ching. His father was about to commit suicide when he was stopped by an immortal. The immortal overpowered Na Cha and bound him up. He then forced Na Cha to promise to live in harmony with his father and to respect him as his father. Na Cha finally, and most reluctantly, agreed to this and was freed. In case he should go back on his promise, the weapon used to subdue him was placed in his father's keeping — It was a golden pagoda.

With familial harmony established, Na Cha and father joined the Chous in their ultimately successful war against the Shang dynasty which fell in 1027 BC. It is "recorded" that in this war he fought against the Star God, Chang Kuei-fang, thirty to forty times without result. In none of them could he be dislodged from his fire wheels which were highly manoeuvrable. Once, he heard this god call his name three times which should have separated his soul from his spirit. It didn't for he subsequently broke Chang Kuei-fang's arm and knocked him off his horse. When asked to explain he told them that he had changed himself into a lotus flower which has neither soul nor spirit. Being made of lotus stalks, this probably wasn't very difficult.

This story is clearly an abridgement of a longer, written account. There is something too complete and detailed about it for it to be properly called a myth, or even a legend. It is probably more correct to call it a fairy story, one which has provided the basis for a great many films, books and songs. He is an extremely popular god. Like Monkey, the Chinese enjoy his naughtiness and are not at all disapproving.

But what kind of God is he? He is not emblematic and therefore necessary. He is not a virtuous official who was subsequently raised to Heaven by Imperial decree. He does not appear to have been a local cult whose popularity spread. His attributes are rather vague but the story does mention that he was given the titles — and therefore the jobs — "Grand Marshall of the Skies" and "Guardian of the Gates of Heaven". Uniquely, according to the story, he was born a God — a reincarnation of a god named Ling Chu-tzu meaning "the intelligent pearl".

This places him in a category of his own — Gods born of human parents.

If we go back to the story, we note that he fought in the dynastic battles that brought the Chous to power. Now this change of dynasty has much the same importance for China as Caesar's invasion of England had for the British. Before that event everything is shadowy, after it we are in contact, however vaguely, with history. Its importance, like the Trojan Wars, is shown by the fact it was a war also of Gods.

During the Shang-Chou conflict there were two Marshalls on the Shang side, Chen Lung and Ch'en Chi, who are familiarly known as Snorter and Blower; Snorter was captured and persuaded to join the Chou army. Eventually he came face to face with Blower, his old comrade, and they fought. They were evenly matched and as no side could gain an advantage other heros joined in. Na Cha wounded Blower in the shoulder and he was finally dispatched by someone else. As Snorter was also killed, they were both later cannonized as temple guardians.

In the eighth century AD, when the Buddhists were establishing themselves, a Singhalese Buddhist Pu K'ung introduced the guardians of Buddhist temples: They were naturalized Chinese citizens and were given the names Mo Li-ch'ing, Mo Li-hai, Mo Li-hung and Mo Li-shou. They guarded the East, West, South and North respectively. They too lived according to legend at the time of the Shang-Chou conflict and were on the side of the Shangs. They too were defeated with the help of Na Cha who fought with Mo Li Ch'ing and broke his jade bracelet — probably indicating that he hit him on his fighting arm and broke his "luck".

These temple guardians are there to prevent evil spirits from taking over — as they are inclined to do. Na Cha however, appears to be able to enter and leave both Taoist and Buddhist temples without too much trouble. He has incapacitated one guardian from each. It may be for this reason that some Buddhist temples also have the image of Li Ching holding a pagoda in his hand. The guardians are good for most evil spirits but for Na Cha, Li Ching is needed. Li Ching has himself been elevated. To some he is the Prime Minister of Heaven, to others he is one of Kuan Ti's assessors.

If this protection is necessary it is clear that Na Cha's status is highly dubious. He is credited with having a mission to rid the world of evil spirits yet he himself is clearly not wholly unblemished.

There is in Sham Shui Po a temple to the third prince, erected, in 1898, by the Hakka community, in gratitude for his having rid them of the plague. On one side of the main altar is an altar to Kuan Yin and on the other an altar to Pao Kung. Effective though Na Cha is, care is taken to see that he is bound by compassion and justice.

The symmetry of his relationship with the guardians of Traditional and Buddhist temples suggests that his importance grew after the eighth century AD. By the time the Emperor Yung Lo, third Ming Emperor, mounted the Imperial throne in 1403, he was probably at the height of his importance for the city of Peking was rebuilt according to the interaction of the five elements and the five viscera and other parts of Na Cha's body, figuratively disposed, with his head to the South.

But was Na Cha a historical person? Was he, like Kuan Ti, a military hero subsequently deified? The answer, not surprisingly, is no. He was, in fact, a Hindu God. This would have been immediately obvious to an expert of Mandarin for the characters used for his name, are one of a series used to transliterate Indian sounds into Chinese. Rather than meaning "Here (or that) is a loud cry (or noise)", the characters – like our own "Aargh!" or "humph" – represent the actual sound of a cry. He has been identified as the son of the Hindu God of Thunder, Visrapani.

Perhaps the earliest reference to him occurs in the biography of an eminent monk called Xuan who lived in the Sung Dynasty. What follows is a translation of this passage:–

Monk Xuan was travelling at night when he fell down. From a terrace in front of him, some being picked him up. His leg was unhurt. Looking at that being, he saw it was a young man – upon which he asked who was there in the dead of the night. The youngster answered, 'I am no ordinary person but none other than Na Cha, the son of the King of Heaven, Bisamen'. Having been instructed in the law, he sustained the monk. That was very long ago.

At first sight this is a rather prosaic story with the only curious element being that the monk instructed the son of a god. The story, however, does not refer to a real journey. "Travelling" was a common expression for meditation and "terraces of the night" a euphemism for the underworld. The God he met was Na Cha (not *Li* Na Cha), son of "Bisamen". This is close to "Visrapani" – but not as close as it could be – Visrapani was, like Avalokitisvara, one of the Buddha's faithful companions. Normally depicted in a terrifying manner and holding a thunderbolt, he is seen as the ideal of the faithful and terror of the impious. Of a son I can find no reference. Na Cha was also at first depicted holding a thunderbolt, but the Chinese could make no symbolic meaning of this and it quickly became a pagoda. Na Cha appears therefore to be Visrapani himself. This is not impossible. "Visrapani" is also spelt "Vajrapani"; "V" and "Jr" are difficult sounds for Chinese and they would probably pronounce it *Wa-ja* (pani). It is also impossible that the nearest equivalent in terms of meaning – for sound without meaning is inconceivable in this context – was "Na Cha".

In Buddhist symbolism the thunderbolt represents the divine force of Buddhist doctrine which shatters all false beliefs and destroys earthly evil.

The dagoba (originally Dagoba) is also of Indian origin; it being the Chinese equivalent of a stupa. Introduced in the third century AD, pagodas were (and still are) built to mark the spot where sacred relics are interred and to protect them. They are also erected to commemorate acts of devotion as well as to secure beneficial influences. The most famous pagoda ever to be erected was built by the Emperor Yung Lo in Nanking. It was known as the porcelain tower and stood for 450 years. We now have two of the elements contained in the later myth: the Pagoda and the Spiritual Teacher of a God. When, then, did Na Cha become Li Na Cha? I have not been able to discover an exact date but there is evidence that it must have been after the time of the Emperor Yung Lo (1403 – 1424). As we have already seen Yung Lo probably considered Na Cha as his patron and in this context the God is always referred to simply as Na Cha.

As I stated earlier the story of Li Na Cha is extremely detailed and curiously complete. There do not seem to be alternative versions of the story, which, to me, looks suspiciously as if the story was created by a single author. If so he must have had a purpose. This may, of course, have been to provide entertainment. Yet, if this is the case then it is a form of entertainment in a category of its own. Creating the biographies of known Gods is not a popular form of literary endeavour.

The Na Cha myth differs from that of Monkey in that it does not seem to have been based on a tradition of folk-tales. It appears to have arrived in a complete form. Interestingly Na Cha features in the myth of Monkey. It is not surprising that these two paragons of irresponsibility, and military prowess, neither really human, should meet in combat. The people would have demanded it. In such a battle who would emerge the victor? What is interesting is that oral memory differs from the record. A friend of mine mentioned the battle and said that Na Cha had won. He said the account of this appears in the novel *Monkey*. There however it is not Na Cha but his elder brother who crosses swords with Monkey-and is soundly beaten. A children's account of the story recently published in China includes an episode in which Na Cha himself engages Monkey but again Monkey wins by transforming himself into a fire-wheel which Na Cha assumes is his own, but when he steps on it he is unceremoniously dumped. The story of a Na Cha victory very probably occurs in one of the spin-off legends attached to him but older sources give Monkey a clear advantage.

When I first read the Na Cha story I took it as a satire on the possibility of Gods being born of men, that is, a satire on Buddhism. Here we have a god, presumably reincarnated for some purpose, forced to commit suicide at the age of seven simply because of the disasters he unintentionally brings on his family. Gods, the story seems to tell us, cannot be filial sons.

I then noted a very curious aspect of the story. It appeared to be in almost every respect the antithesis of the Miao Shan legends. Kuan Yin's name is "The Hearer of the Cries of the World"; his name is "Here is a loud cry". She is the third daughter of a legendary king, he is the third son. She saves the third prince of the sea dragon, he kills the third prince of the sea dragon. They are both at some time immured behind stone walls and both are "killed" by the father destroying the stone walls by burning them down. Kuan Yin subsequently saves her father. Na Cha tries to kill his father. Throughout her agency, Kuan Yin is compassionate whereas Na Cha is noted for his total lack of compassion. There may also be a correspondence in the fact that Kuan Yin was the recipient of a pearl given to her so that she could study the scriptures at night, while Na Cha is a reincarnation of "The Intelligent Pearl".

The consistency of the antithesis between the Na Cha and Miao Shan myths forces me to believe that the former is a hidden satire on the latter. But who would write such a satire? The obvious culprits would be the Taoists who were continually waging campaigns against the Buddhists yet this cannot be for Na Cha's surname "Li" is also the surname of Lao Tzu who, according to the myth, chose Li Erh (Plum Ear) as his name when he was born. No Taoist would put himself in the position of inviting a satirical riposte. Could it be a Confucian? Then why make the Taoist immortal central to the story? I don't think the idea that the myth is a satire of one philosophy by upholders of another, stands up. We must look for another victim.

We have already noted that the Emperor Yung Lo, third emperor of the Ming Dynasty, was Buddhist in inclination and that Na Cha was especially favoured by him. At this time Na Cha was not associated with the surname Li, yet by the time, "Monkey" was written (1570?) the myth had been created and had also become entwined with the Monkey legends for he appears in the novel — albeit as a very minor figure. Somewhere between 1403 and 1570 (?), the story was created.

Li is a surname with imperial associations for it was the family name of the emperors of the T'ang Dynasty. It is unlikely that someone writing during or after Yung Lo's reign would have found much satisfaction in attacking the emperors of 500 years before. Satire is more concerned with contemporary events. However, by choosing the name of one imperial family the author may have been pointing an oblique finger at another – a necessary precaution if the butt of the satire was still occupying the throne. If Na Cha was the patron of Yung Lo, what better way could there be of satirizing the man than through a mock biography of the God.

Yung Lo was the fourth son of the founder of the Ming Dynasty, Hung-wu (1368–1398) and was probably not born of the Empress but of a concubine. Despite this lack of status in the imperial household he was clearly a man of ability and this was recognized by his father for he was given significantly more responsibility than any of his other brothers with the sole exception of the third son. At the age of ten he was made Prince of Yen (Peking – then the city controlling the Northern frontier). He took up residence there when he was 20, but it was not until he was 33 in 1393 that he took over the full powers associated with the title. By 1398 when Hung-wu died he was the eldest surviving son but the heir to the throne was the teenage son of Yung Lo's eldest brother. Yung Lo nevertheless pressed his own, strong, claims to the throne and when these were ignored, he rose in revolt. After four years of fighting, he captured Nanking, one of the two capitals of China – the other being Ch'ang An. His nephew, the Emperor Chien-wen, either died or as legend asserts, disappeared and became a Buddhist monk. When Yung Lo took over, history was rewritten to portray the events in a light favourable to the new Emperor.

Are there any correlations between this career and the details of the myth? In my opinion there is sufficient to give the idea plausibility. A boy born in 1393 would be seven years old in 1398, according to Chinese reckoning. When Na Cha was seven years old he was six foot tall i.e. a "big" man. When he was seven he entered the waters and made them boil so shaking the Sea Dragon's temple. The dragon is prime symbol of the emperor, so the temple would be the ancestral shrine of the imperial family. Here we have a very clear metaphor for revolt. The temple was shaken but did not break, which is to say the rebel was of the same family but that the ancestors were displeased with him for ignoring the accepted rules of inheritance. Na Cha fought forty bouts with Ao-ping – does this refer to the four years it took for Yung Lo to win the war of succession? Finally he stripped the scales off the Dragon King's body as well as from the body of Ao-ping i.e. – he took by force the imperial insignia and vestments.

There is a neat opposition of ideas in that Na Cha is the "Third Prince" while Ao-ping means the third fish tail. Yung Lo was the third emperor while Chien-wen was the pre-eminent heir of the third generation, being the eldest son of the eldest son — (the third tail of the imperial fish?)

So far we have not had to do too much damage to the facts but what are we to make of Na Cha's suicide, his immurement and the other events? We can push a little further ahead. When the Prince of Yen took over the empire he ceased to be. Instead, he became that semi-deity, the Son of Heaven, Emperor of China, the Emperor Yung Lo. As we know Peking was laid out according to certain specifications related to the idealized body of Na Cha. His "head" was placed facing South to indicate life for the dead were always laid with the head to the North. It was Yung Lo who made Peking the capital of China and the building of the city was a massive project which, on completion, drew to it a large population. Work started in 1407 and the city was completed in 1421 when the capital was officially moved, though Yung Lo had been in residence there since 1417. It was an immensely difficult process fraught with problems of organization, transport and labour. It was also expensive. The burden on the tax payer was oppressive. There was also widespread discontent among the bureaucrats who resisted the change of capitals.

In 1421 a fire broke out and destroyed the main audience halls of the Palace. This was not only inauspicious but hit at the heart of the political sensitivity. Yung Lo called for frank criticism and then executed the most outspoken of the critics — one Hsiao Yi. The pavilions were never rebuilt by Yung Lo.

Not only does this final episode give us one more corroborative element, it also shows that an important section of the administration were disenchanted with Yung Lo. It is to this section of the community that we would naturally look for an author of a satire and their disaffection provides the cause.

All along I have assumed satirical intent to the story yet its true purpose may have been more complex. Na Cha's absurdity and irresponsibility in the first half of the story gives way to a more mature anger in the second half as Na Cha attempts to revenge himself on his father, followed by military heroism in the subsequent dynastic war. Yung Lo personally led five military campaigns against Northern tribes, dying on his return from the last at the age of 64. Nor can I ignore the fact that the Taoist immortal says at the beginning of the story "Woman, receive the child of a unicorn". The unicorn, along with the tortoise, phoenix and dragon is one of the four great mythical creatures and is a creature of good omen. It symbolizes grandeur, loyalty, faithfulness, wise administration, longevity, potency and illustrious offspring. This may, of course, have been included to highlight the satire that follows. It may also have been evidence of an ambivalent attitude or might it not simply have been the author's escape clause if his authorship had been discovered.

If I am right in thinking the story was a satire it would have circulated only among a small circle of friends at first and not published perhaps for some years. The Chinese have a long tradition of oblique satire and how a satire can be completely misconstrued is nicely revealed by the following episode.

On the first anniversary of Mao Tse-tung's birthday, there was a riot in T'ien An Men Square. Not long afterwards a story began to circulate. This story went like this:

A farmer on a commune went to examine the rice fields and came upon a small area that had been completely destroyed. He assumed it had been trampled by a water buffalo and made sure the animal in question was securely tethered. The next day he again inspected the patch and to his horror discovered that the damage had become much greater. Not knowing who or what was responsible he spent the following night in vigil. At midnight he heard a noise and looking closely saw that frogs had appeared. They formed two battle lines and using rice stalks, which they pulled out from the ground, they attacked each other. When morning came they cleared away the dead and disappeared.

This, a satire on the T'ien An Men events, attacked the factionalism that was threatening people's livelihoods — their rice. The story spread like wildfire and was widely believed in its literal form. Popular anxiety was such that the Canton authorities made it a punishable offence to even mention the story.

A satire does not have to be too distanced from its intended victim for it to be taken as gospel. Could this not have been the rather ironical fate of the Li Na Cha story?

Tin Hau:
Queen of Heaven

It is a relief to get away from the fanciful stories that grace the pages of the last three chapters. While folk legends will appear in future chapters they do so as descriptions of isolated incidents illustrating the powers possessed by the God involved. They are also far more earth bound. They relate to the common people and the problems that beset them.

The story of Tin Hau's earthly existence and the subsequent history of her cult have an almost classical simplicity, epitomizing the pattern of deification.

The future Goddess was born on the island of Mei Chou in Fukien province, possibly from 900 AD – 1,000 AD. She was the daughter of a minor official and her full name was Lin Ma-tzu.

It would appear that even before the major event of her earthly life she was considered to be a bit strange. She was a devotee of Kuan Yin and refused to marry.

One day she went into a trance and dreamt that there would be a storm and that it would destroy all the boats in the fleet. Running down to the beach she pointed fixedly at her father's boat which, when the storm suddenly blew up, was the only one to be saved. This story, no doubt, appeals to inshore fishermen. For deep sea fishermen the story goes that in her trance she saw that the storm had already hit and that the fleet was in trouble. In spirit she arrived at the scene and began to lead her brothers to safety. Her mother, however, seeing her daughter in a trance, shook her violently and managed to bring her out of her dream state. Ma-tzu berated her for this, saying that she had been brought back to earth too soon.

No one understood the significance of this until three of her four brothers returned – one variation has all the brothers returning but without the father. The survivors explained that each of their ships had been led to safety by the image of a girl who they now recognized as their sister.

So far, it seems, so good and yet we already have an apparent inconsistency. What is a minor official doing fishing? This can be explained if we assume that the father was clearly wealthy, each of his sons had his own boat, and that, because of his influence, the magistrate had designated to him some function such as that of tax collector. This would be one way of getting round the problem yet it doesn't convince me. It is my feeling that the story and the association with the Lin clan have different but equally strong origins. The Lin clan on the island of Mei Chou are recorded as calling her "auntie" and leaving their children in her temple while they work in the fields. The Lin aspect of the story cannot be avoided.

The story relating her miraculous rescue would seem to be of later origin. Sung Dynasty records refer only to four facts: that she was from Mei Chou; that she was of the Lin family; that she was versed in fortune telling and that after she died she was worshipped.

Ma-tzu died at the age of twenty-eight, after she had perfected her religious powers, and became a supernatural being who often helped those in danger on the sea. 28 is the number of Hsiu, the divisions of the Chinese universe.

Her worship did not however start for some time after her death. It appears that the people of Mei Chou were lax in according her dues and it was not until many years later that one night she appeared to all the inhabitants of Mei Chou in a dream. To each of them she said: "I am the Goddess of Mei Chou. I must be given a dwelling here." This is the story as inscribed in a temple in Hangchou in 1228. Hangchou is in the north of Chekiang province.

Her first substantial "miracle" occurred in 1122 when she is credited with saving an imperial official who was on an embassy to Korea. The official, Lu Yun-ti by name, told the emperor of his salvation and "The Temple of the Fortunate Crossing" was set up in her honour. This act amounts to canonization. The mission was clearly an important one — probably aimed at an alliance. The tribes in the north were fighting among themselves and the emperor may have decided that this was a good time to strengthen his position.

The capital of China at this time was K'aifeng. An embassy from K'aifeng to Korea would not have gone through Fukien. Clearly, even by 1122, without the benefits of canonization, the cult of Ma-tzu had spread North along the coast of China. It also seems to have spread

South. There is a story that in 1012 two members of the Lin family were shipwrecked on Tung Lung Island and built a temple to her. Their descendants were responsible for building the original temple in Joss House Bay in 1266 and even now descendants of these Lins receive $200 a year from the Chinese Temples Committee.

Once canonized her promotion was rapid. In 1155 she was decreed Princess of Supernatural Favour; in 1192 she became Queen; in 1198 Holy Queen and in 1278 Kublai Khan decreed her Queen of Heaven, equal to Kuan Ti, and, by implication, subordinate only to the Jade Emperor. Tin Hau means Queen of Heaven. Even at this exalted height there was still room for further promotion. The first Ch'ing Emperor raised her from Imperial Concubine to Imperial Consort.

The story behind this is worth relating. When the Manchus invaded China their progress was impeded by supporters of the Mings. One of these supporters was Cheng Ch'eng-kung, known at the time as Kao Hsing-yeh, which was transmuted into Koxinga by the Dutch. Koxinga was hemmed in by the Ch'ing armies in the Amoy region. He rationalized his position by taking to his ships and invading Taiwan, then in the hands of the Dutch. His victory he credited to Ma-tzu's support. When the Ch'ings attacked Taiwan 21 years later they too claimed to have received support from Ma-tzu. Perhaps it is this reputation for impartiality that has caused Ma-tzu to be represented in her statues with a black face. Another explanation is that as her element is water she is associated with the North the colour of which is black.

The rapidity of her promotion under the Sungs is unprecedented. Over a period of 76 years she was raised in status four times. It took only 156 years for her to rise from being a coastal cult figure to achieve the highest rank available to a woman. Why? We can only conjecture.

It is possible that the Taoists wanted to create a Goddess whose popularity would overshadow that of Kuan Yin. If so they failed for she was incorporated into the myth. Perhaps it was the Buddhists who insinuated the detail that Ma-tzu as a girl was a devotee of Kuan Yin.

Another reason may have been that China was divided in two; the Sungs who ruled the South were separated from the Kins in the North by the waters of the Yangtze River. In sea-craft alone were the Sungs superior to their northern neighbours and Ma-tzu's importance may be an idealized reflection of this state of affairs. Again the internal crisis in China may have allowed piracy a free reign, making sea voyages more perilous.

Kublai Khan's promotion of her is more interesting for it occurred two years after he had occupied Hangchou and a year before the last Sung Emperor died. Kublai Khan was then, in the middle of a military campaign and the indications are that it was a political act. Fukien is a highly mountainous region and its inhabitants have always looked outwards to the sea for communication with the outside world. Kublai Khan, being a Mongol, was, in any case, favourably disposed to Goddesses and evidently he hoped by this act of promotion to gain favour with the Fukienese. He in fact bypassed Fukien province and did not take it over until 1283, that is to say three years after he had taken on the mantle of emperor and five years after the promotion of Ma-tzu. Although he was not yet an emperor the promotion stands justified by subsequent events.

I find the last promotion, again by a northern tribe and again with obvious political overtones, to be slightly problematic. For the first time in Chinese mythology a Goddess is clearly identified as having a sexual function. This last promotion is not often referred to in the literature nor, I believe, is it widely known by those who worship at her temples. Virginity, while going against the grain, is for some reason essential to a Goddess. If virginity is out of the question then chastity and fecundity are the basis, not just necessary conditions of respect. Only a virgin who has foresworn marriage can be unselfish and dispassionate in her relations with other women. Only a virgin can treat men with equal concern. The title of Queen, is rightly imprecise as to the true nature of the position. Concubine and Consort are too precise. They give rise to the possibility, seemingly alien to Chinese imagination, that the Gods can produce children in Heaven.

Whatever her titles she is most commonly known by her given name Ma-tzu. Ma-tzu means maternal grandmother. It is hard to believe that a baby girl would be given this name Lin Ma-tzu. Maternal grandmother of the Lin family, suggests either the matriarchal head of a clan or a Goddess of the forest — the surname Lin (林) means forest. Boats being made of wood, was she worshipped originally as the spirit who gave strength to boats at times of danger? Earth is female. It is more credible to see her as the personified Goddess of the earth in whose realm lie the Yellow Springs — source of water and of life.

It is as Goddess of the waters that she is worshipped and many are the stories of her saving those at sea. It is said that when everything is black, when the wind is up and the sea is high, when everything is obscured, a light appears at the tip of the mast. This is the fire of Ma-tzu and should it ever leave the ship will meet with disaster.

In temples to her, there are two subordinate and grotesque figures. Their names are Thousand League Eyes and Favouring Wind Ears. As with all attendants, they manifest attributes pertaining to their superior. Like other guardians their origins are imputed to the dynastic wars between the Chou and Shang. For some reason the glass picture has omitted them and replaced them with two girl attendants. This emphasises her imperial status to the detriment of her saving powers.

A Goddess whose main attribute is that she saves the lives of sailors poses problems. The Chinese also believe that the length of one's life is fixed at birth and that what is written down in the register of death cannot be changed. Now, consistency is not to be expected yet it seems to me that an awareness of this problem has brought about a blurring of identities. Tou Mou, the Goddess of Measure, is sometimes said to be an aspect of Tin Hau.

Tou Mou is usually represented with many arms and a caste mark on her forehead, strongly suggesting Indian origins. Of these origins little or nothing is known. Her Chinese story goes like this:

> There was once a beautiful maiden who attained a profound knowledge of celestial mysteries. She shone with a heavenly light and could trip over the waves without getting her feet wet — in this way she managed to save many lives. The King of North China heard of her many virtues and great wisdom, so he took her as his wife. She produced nine sons for him. When the time came for her to pass over into the other world, the Lord of Heaven himself invited her to live in the palace of the pole star. She was made the pivot of the pole and given the title Queen of the Doctrine of Primitive Heaven. Her third eye in her forehead allows her to see everything. If prayed to, she had the power to prolong life. Her nine sons, who became the first human sovereigns to succeed the celestial sovereigns, reside on neighbouring stars and pay her homage.

There are several echoes of the Ma-tzu legend at the beginning: the bright light and the ability to save men from drowning but apart from these the idea of the deity appears to be very different.

At funerals, one of the officiants, whether Buddhist or Taoist — I have seen both — sits on a raised lotus throne made out of wood and paper. In this posture he is standing in for Tou Mou.

The three eyes, the lotus throne and the association with the constant law of the universe — she is the pivot of the pole — suggest a connection with the Hindu pole star deity — Dhruma Lok a prince who meditated in order to discover Lotus Eyes (?). Once started he never stopped and the universe created itself around him. Appeal is made to him to intercede with the God Abathur who weighs the deeds of departed spirits.

If this is the origin more questions are raised than answered.

It is more commonly believed that she derived from the Hindu Goddess, Marici, who is Goddess of the Dawn and whose name means "she who radiates light". It is possible, of course, that Tou Mou derives from a combination of the two.

Tou Mou is also mentioned in one of the Miao Shan legends. When Miao Shan went to the nunnery, her father ordered that she be given all the most menial tasks. Tou Mou took pity on her and ordered the animal kingdom to help her and so ease her burden.

The extent to which Chinese Goddesses interact with each other contrasts with the lack of this among the Gods.

Tam Kung:
The Boy God

At the end of the praya of Coloane Town in Macau there is a small temple to Tam Kung. Inside there is a rib from a whale to which someone has added a number of small wooden carvings, transforming it into a replica of a dragon boat. Whale bones are also very much in evidence at a temple to Ho Wang in Tai O, on the southern tip of Lantau Island. This temple is delightfully sited on a tongue of land almost entirely surrounded by water. The two Gods honoured by these temples are intimately connected for they died within seconds of each other just over seven hundred years ago.

In 1276 Kublai Khan's Mongol troops swept south of the Yangtze river and took Hangchou, capital of the southern Sung dynasty. They captured the emperor – no more than a boy – and took him to Peking. The emperor's younger brothers managed to escape and they fled south. The next eldest was invested with the mantle of Son of Heaven and became the focus of Sung resistance to the invaders. The speed of the Mongol advance bogged down, literally, in the rice country of the south but they remained irresistible, continuing to force their way south. The new emperor died and the mantle fell on the youngest of the brothers – an eight-year-old child. Finally, in 1278 or 1279 (accounts vary), what little remained of the Sung court found themselves on a rocky island off Kwangtung province surrounded by the Mongols. There was no hope of escape. One of the chief ministers took the young boy on his shoulders and leapt off a cliff. Both drowned but death was honourable.

Such are the bare facts around which a rather more eleborate story has been strung. According to this, the boy emperor arrived in Hongkong harbour with an imperial fleet of junks carrying some three thousand soldiers, retainers and ministers. They landed on Kowloon peninsula roughly where Kai Tak airport now is. They were met by the villagers of the place whose headman – one Tam Kung – welcomed them and did their best to provision them. The emperor built a house on a small hill overlooking what is now Kowloon City. They did not stay long but sailed across the pearl river estuary to Heungshan, where rice was more plentiful. Shortly after this the Mongol fleet caught up with them. The two fleets clashed and the Sung fleet was scattered and destroyed. Lo So Fu, the chief minister, ordered his wife and daughter to drown themselves while he took the emperor on his shoulders and jumped into the water.

The story incidentally gives the origin of the name Kowloon to the fact that the emperor counted the peaks and commented that there were eight dragons but was reminded that since he was present there were nine. Kowloon means nine dragons.

The historical accuracy of this slightly more elaborate account is suspect but it is quite likely that the last Sung Emperor did set foot on Kowloon peninsula. Tradition is obstinate. When the Japanese took Hong Kong they decided to expand the airport. Unfortunately a hill stood in the way. This hill was traditionally the site of a large cave where the Sung Emperor resided while his boats were being repaired. Before work started on blasting the hill away the Japanese carried out a ceremony involving fifty Japanese monks to persuade the spirit of the Sung Emperor to find another residence.

If Tam Kung were a popular God throughout China we would be fairly safe in dismissing the story but he is not. He is a God confined to a very small area — the coastal strip that includes Hong Kong and Macau. This adds some credibility to the legend though there are details that one should take with a pinch of salt. It is said the young emperor had never seen lychees before his arrival. When he saw them they were unripe. He sighed and exclaimed that he would have liked to taste them. The next day the lychee tree he had been looking at was heavy with red ripe fruit. There is even a plaque at the spot where this is supposed to have occurred in Heungshan, north of Macau.

Putting the pieces together it is clear that Tam Kung is the last Sung Emperor deified under another name. There is no ambiguity about the identification. Tam Kung is a boy. He is a God of local provenance and he is prayed to for safety at sea. Ho Wang also is a wholly local figure and it is explicitly stated that he was an officer in the Emperor's retinue and that he jumped off a cliff with the boy Emperor.

Why is the boy God called Tam Kung? The extended account of the history adds the detail that Tam Kung, who we are told was the headman of a village where Kowloon City now is, began to be remembered at a time when the power of the Mongols was waning. The answer is now clear. He was worshipped under another name as it would be rather foolhardy to admit to worshipping the last Sung Emperor when the Mongols were in power. Worship went underground until it was safe to emerge, early in the Ming Dynasty. But why was he given the surname Tam? We can be sure that he was not given — or lent — the name of a village headman. It would be sacriligious to name an emperor after a mere peasant. It is also unlikely that a village headman would have been called Lord Tam. Kung, Lord, is an honourific title normally only accorded to the elderly and the wealthy. The Tam Kung of the story was neither. Tam, (譚), is a common enough surname and has the additional meaning of "to boast". The character is made up of "word" (言), "west", (西), and (早), which can either mean "early morning" or "long ago". As west is the direction of old age and dying there appears to be the implication "the world of the old ancestors".

Given this, Tam seems to be a fairly appropriate name to bequeath a recently dead emperor, the worship of whom must be kept secret. Further support that we are on the right track can be gained from looking at a closely related word. Tam, (禫), is identical in tone, in Cantonese, to the surname and as we can see by comparing the characters, the two "Tams" share a similar range of reference. This word is the name of the sacrifice made at the end of the 27-month period of mourning for a parent. The emperor was considered the father and mother of the people.

Having said all this, the identification of Tam Kung with the boy Sung Emperor is not as widely acknowledged as perhaps it should be. Burckhardt makes no mention of the connection. He gives us only the unsatisfactory information that he was a local worthy hailing from Wei Yang, a Hakka district in Kwangtung, who attained enlightenment in Kowloon and who derived his powers from the petrified remains of the nine dragons that form the northern boundary of Kowloon. Another story says that he was worshipped as a God when he was 12 years old. All stories however assert that he has power over rain and water and is very efficacious when it comes to extinguishing fires. His celebrations take place on the eighth day of the fourth moon, which is the beginning of summer.

The insistent connection with dragons, the imperial symbol, seems to bolster our original claims that he is the deification of the last Sung Emperor. As an ancestor his element would be water while the element associated with summer is fire. Winter is the dry season. By the beginning of summer the earth is parched. If the harvest is to be good rain must fall. He is very good at extinguishing fire. It is said that he could summon rain by throwing a cup of water in the air. As water flows under the earth it must get into the sky somehow.

The picture is neat but not as neat as it would be if we insisted that his imperial origins had precedence over his powers to control rain. The dragon is the animal symbol of the third month denoting the end of spring. Tin Hau, whose feast is on the 23rd day of this month, clearly has precedence both in the matter of making rain and in her claims to imperial insignia. Tam Kung has to be content with the snake — son of the dragon and one of the two animals of winter.

If any readers of this book wish to collect glass paintings of the Gods they will find it difficult to find one of Tam Kung. I was forced to commission the one I possess, which explains the relative crudity of its execution. The woman in the shop asked me how I wished the painting to depict him. Did I want him standing with an arm in the air, feet on whirling discs? We discussed his stance for ten minutes until an inner voice advised me to establish his normal posture. He is always seated and holds a bell in one hand they told me. So be it. But why the bell? I asked. They shrugged. Because he is a boy and boys play with bells, one suggested. The handbell was used to instruct soldiers to stand still and be silent and for this reason became associated with veneration and respect. Bells of this sort have been used since antiquity by heralds of the sovereign to convene assemblies to hear the Imperial messages. Tam Kung holds the bell calling us to hear the word of the ancestors.

San Chou Niang Niang:
Mother of the Three Islands

This enigmatic lady, adorned with the yellow cloak that signifies imperial status and holding the septre of an empress, stared down at me for over a year, smiling her mysterious half-smile, while I tried to avoid the problem of who she was. None of my basic reference books seemed to have heard of her. One day, while meditating on the problem of what islands were referred to, I picked up *Outlines of Chinese Symbolism*, opened it and found myself faced with the entry on "The Islands of the Blest" which starts — "The three islands. . . ." When one is dealing with Gods coincidences like this take on an extra dimension.

The Islands of the Blest are the mythical dwelling place of the immortals and are popularly supposed to be situated to the east of Kiangsu Province. Here, immortals live in marvellous mansions, drink from the invigorating fountain of life — a fountain which springs from a jade-stone rock — and eat the pearls along the shore and the mushroom of immortality.

As we have already seen the idea of immortality is really an extension of the idea that long life equals great virtue. If one can extend one's life, one has proved the greatness of one's virtue. Different schools of thought attempted to solve the problem of obtaining immortality in various ways. Some worked through alchemy, while others desisted from eating grain. From 400 BC onwards, this obsession with immortality grew increasingly stronger. They based their beliefs, where they could, in the writings of the philosophical Taoists. It is in the works of Chuang Tzu (fourth century BC) and Lieh Tzu who (predated him) that we first hear of Spiritualized Man, Realized Man, magic islands, the magic powers of the inhabitants and the Isles of the Blest. On these islands the buildings are of gold and all living creatures are white. Here is the basis of the idea from which the myth of the immortals grew. Chuang Tzu and Lieh Tzu would probably turn in their graves if they knew. It is unlikely that they intended these concepts to be taken literally. These early immortals were clearly Hygienists and Proto-alchemists in concept. They were magic fairies, uncountable in number, who possessed magic recipes and foods. Given their reality it is not surprising that expeditions were then organized to find them. The first recorded expedition was in the fourth century BC. The most spectacular expedition was launched by Ch'in Shih Huang Ti (221–260 BC) who equipped one led by a magician Hsu Fu and carrying 3,000 young men and girls. Despite the failure of these expeditions — they claimed to have caught sight of the islands but were blown off course by contrary winds — the first Ch'in Emperor continued in his search for immortality. He had 270 palaces built, connected by covered ways so that no one could see where he slept. He also used to travel frequently to the coast where he hoped to catch a glimpse of the blessed isles and it was here that he died. Legend stated that a monster, or giant fish, barred the way to the islands and that Ch'in Shih Huang Ti killed it with an arrow upon which act his soul was immortalized, leaving his body.

The idea of the Eight Immortals who act as a Taoist pantheon only came about during the Yuan Dynasty, though the individuals involved have a longer history. Some say that they existed as a body during the Sung Dynasty which seems more likely. This body of immortals seems to have arisen to provide the Taoist counterpart of a similar body which was Buddhist — the Eighteen Arhats. "Arhatship implies possession of certain supernatural powers, and is not to be succeeded by Buddhaship, but implies the fact of the saint having already attained Nirvana." Saint, Immortal, Arhat — all occupy much the same spiritual space within their different systems though they do not seem to share the same function. The saint is primarily an intercessor; the arhat, a protector of the system while the immortal seems to have very little exalted purpose. One explanation of the immortals is that each represents a different condition of life — poverty, wealth, aristocracy, the commoner, age, youth, masculinity and femininity. However, it is not easy to match the individuals and their associations.

These immortals are only occasionally connected to the Three Islands of the Blest. I discovered these three islands occurring in a strange context when I visited the Kuan Yin Temple in Tainan (Taiwan). There the God, Wei To, a common temple guardian — also called Veda — had the characters 三洲感應 , meaning the sixth sense of the three islands, above his statue. This was a temple attached to a Buddhist nunnery. Immortals in a Buddhist temple? I asked a nun what islands they were but she didn't know. I looked at the wall behind her and saw a picture of Jesus Christ.

These three islands are ruled over by "Mother". This Goddess is also called the Jade Lady or Heavenly Mother. The Empresses of China were also respectfully addressed as "Mother" — which no doubt explains our lady's imperial garb. Unfortunately apart from her name we know little about her. No earthly existence seems to have been credited to her. In addition there seem to be a variety of goddesses similarly referred to as Mothers.

There is a body known as the "nine dark ladies" composed of Mothers. They all seem to be protecting divinities. Thus Yen Kuang Niang Niang cures opthalmia — a disease that used to be prevalent in the North of China; Sao Ching Niang Niang sweeps away the clouds when too much rain threatens the crops and Tzu Sun Niang Niang provides children, especially sons. This latter is credited with a biography which states that she was the wife of a virtuous official who provided her husband with five sons and two daughters and then committed suicide rather than yield to an over-ardent prince. She was canonized for her chastity. Her presence at weddings is symbolized by the eating of special cakes by both bride and groom — and it is to her shrine that couples go to pray for children. One of her shrines is a rock on Bowen Road in Hong Kong Island, which is commonly known as Yin Yang stone. Of the other dark ladies I have no information.

Is Mother one of these nine ladies or is she the unity of them all? This second possibility is not as strange as it may seem as is illustrated by the following episode which occurs in the *Romance of the Three Kingdoms*. It is a story found in many other contexts as well.

There was one Kuan Lu, a reader of mystical signs, who saw a young man tilling the fields and knew immediately that this boy only had a few more days to live. Kuan warned him to prepare himself. When the father heard the news he begged Kuan to help them avert this fate and Kuan eventually agreed to do so. He told the boy to prepare some food and take it to a place in the woods where he would find two men playing chess. He was not to disturb them but simply offer the food and stay quiet until they had finished, at which time he was to request them to extend his life. Everything went according to plan and his fate was avoided. The two men were the Gods of the two constellations the Southern and Northern Measures who between them rule over birth and death.

"But the Northern Dipper consists of nine stars and there was only one man," objected the lad.

"Separately they are nine but they combine to form one," Kuan Lu replied.

The concept of the Heavenly Mother is vague and we must not push too hard to make her image more concrete. She may or may not be the unity, she may or may not be connected to the other Mothers, but when she is worshipped she is usually accompanied by at least one of them which suggests a connection of sorts.

It may be that the Jade Lady, possessor of all possible beneficient attributes was too general when it came to dealing with particular problems and so Mothers who dealt with more specific spheres of operation came into being — the most popular of which pertained to posterity.

The Heavenly Mother was canonized during the Sung Dynasty apparently to combat the great popularity that Kuan Yin enjoyed though she may have been promoted to complement the Jade Emperor. If the former theory is true the attempt was a failure. Kuan Yin is unassailable. If one is set up to oppose her she absorbs her opponent into an aspect of her own myth. How this is done can be seen in the following story which is a late version of the Miao Shan legends:

There was a Commissioner named Kuo who had been about to acquire a delicious young girl as his fifth concubine, but the girl had run off an hour before she was due to arrive at his house. He summoned his nephew, a promising young scholar, to set out after her and bring her back. The nephew was reluctant to take the commission but he repressed his sympathy for the girl by calling to mind the Confucian ethics of filial piety which demanded that he obey his uncle. He set out in the direction that the girl had fled and after several days arrived at the temple-dotted slopes of a mountain. It was evening and the girl was, he felt, nearby. Considering it better to wait till the next day, he decided to pass the night in a temple dedicated to Niang Niang.

That night he had a dream in which the Goddess appeared. When he awoke he remembered her words "Listen and obey. Know that, times without number, century after century, I have appeared among men sometimes as now with a celestial body composed of light, sometimes as a human being and more than once as a noble horse. Often I have been manifest in a number of guises simultaneously in several of the innumerable world systems. Known by many names, among them Niang Niang and Kuan Yin, I have often suffered mutilation sooner than accept impious embraces for, as far back as the middle era of a previous world system, I vowed myself to chastity lest my power to mitigate suffering be impaired. If that deluded being, your uncle, has his way, my vow will come to nought and with it will be shattered my power to save myriads of beings as yet unborn. Therefore I have chosen you as the instrument to accomplish my purpose smoothly."

The next morning, putting aside this vision the nephew found the girl and attempted to take her by reason and the power of a warrant he was carrying. Once again she manifested herself and the nephew, now contrite set her free and himself joined a monastery. "In a flash the effects of twenty years of Confucian training had been dissipated by the power of this radiant being."

Niang Niang, manifestation of Kuan Yin, is also fused with Tin Hau. In one village in the New Territories there is a shrine to Tin Hau under the name Ma Niang (媽娘) or Nurse Mother. This "confusion" is a natural reaction to having Heaven populated not only by a Queen of Heaven but also a Mother (Empress) of Heaven. It is strange that Niang Niang has not been totally fused with one or the other for she is otherwise seemingly characterless with the sole function of presiding over the immortals. In this fact lies the vital clue to her identity for this is also the function of the Queen of Western Heaven, Hsi Wang Mu.

We have met her already in connection with the Lao Tzu myth and had a glimpse of her in the Monkey legend. She is one of the oldest Gods of Chinese conception and her origin is often imputed to Lieh Tzu in whose writings she first appears as "Golden Mother of the Tortoise". Lieh Tzu is usually credited with a highly fertile imagination for, as we have seen, much of the myth of immortality first finds expression through his pen. Is it not much more likely that he is commenting on mythological concepts already accepted by the people at large? It is more than probable that the Queen of Western Heaven was conceived by the popular imagination prior to Lieh Tzu's time, if not as a wholly distinct being at least as a personalized force of nature. As a potent figure she gradually acquired individuality, human form and a place in Heaven.

There is a theory that she started life as a plague Goddess and that she was the original Director of Destinies. She observed man and, taking into account the quality of his virtue, bestowed on him the requisite life span. As the progenitors of Taoism became more and more obsessed with the idea of immortality her image became inverted. Instead of visiting death on the non-virtuous she had the power to grant long life — even "Long life no death" — which was how the idea of an immortal existence was expressed — to the virtuous.

Later she was seen as the embodiment of the *Yin* principle who, by interacting with the male principle of the East, gave birth to Heaven and Earth or, as it is sometimes said, nine sons and twenty-four daughters. The nine sons are the nine divisions of the Lo Shu "magic" square and the 24 daughters are the number of intersecting lines.

She lives in a palace in the K'un Lun Mountains, where a variety of red jade is supposed to grow on trees, and is accompanied by five "Jade Ladies" who correspond to the five points of the compass. We remember that Kuan Yin in the story above objected to being the fifth concubine. This gives the story an added layer of meaning suggesting that she did not wish to be incorporated in the Taoist pantheon as one of Hsi Wang Mu's five jade ladies as she was the prior being and Niang Niang was merely one of her manifestations.

In her palace, there is a peach garden where the peaches blossomed once every 3,000 years and ripened for another 3,000 years. It was over this garden that Monkey was, for a short time, given responsibility. In her palace too live the immortals who at other times reside in hills and springs and are really the embodiments in human guise of the spirits who were thought from earliest antiquity to inhabit these places. Humanized they created another layer of being for the ancient, unpersonified, spirits of rocks, trees and streams are still accorded their dues.

Hsi Wang Mu travels on a crane which is symbolic of longevity. The image of a crane is often incorporated into the funeral rites — the effigy of the dead being placed on it so that the crane will take the soul to Heaven. This is a rather later conception of the after-life than the idea of the soul descending to the Yellow Springs under the earth.

She is credited with two earthly visitations. One that we have already mentioned — to Emperor Mu in 985 BC — was an early attempt to prove that he was imbued with the Mandate of Heaven. Clearly this story would only have come into existence when the virtue of the Chou Emperors was in doubt from 650 BC onwards. The other was when the Emperor Wu Ti (140–86 BC) visited her palace. This Emperor was the foil of a number of alchemists and immortality was his sole aim in life. That such a visit should be attached to his name is best seen as alchemistic propaganda.

Hsi Wang Mu's palace has been sited in the Hindu Kush by those who see the "western" aspect of her being as relating to an historical event — either Western influence in the form of the Queen of Sheba or the transmigration of the Chinese people from that quarter somehow retained in the communal memory. As there is no evidence of contact with the Queen of Sheba or of a transmigration of the Chinese race from the west we must look elsewhere. The west, as we know, is the quarter associated with autumn — the season that mediates between the life-dominated summer and the death-dominated winter. It is therefore associated with old age, the autumn of one's years, and with dying. The forces of the universe that are strong at this time of the year govern these processes. As autumn marks the beginning of *Yin's* ascendance in the yearly cycle, these celestial forces are female. A Mother Ruler of the West who governs the length of one's life is the not unlikely result, given these underlying concepts. It is for similar reasons that special attention is paid by Buddhists to the Buddha of Western Paradise.

Hsi Wang Mu is also Golden Mother of the Tortoise. In one sense this is a restating of the idea that she gave birth to the universe, for it is supported by this animal. As the Tortoise is also the Dark Warrior of the North and thus of winter and death, we have the additional idea of death being born from dying just as autumn gives birth to winter. Even today a common inscription on funeral gifts is "May the soul return to the Western Heaven". White, the colour of West, is also that of mourning. The association of white with death is shared by many diverse cultures such as the Jews and the natives of the Andaman Islands in the Indian Ocean. White is also the colour of semen, and thus of life. If semen is seen as the spirit of life, then on death it is this spirit that leaves. We have already noted the division of souls into the male and female of which the former is higher. It is this soul that departs first. The sun sets in the West. *Yang,* and life, gives way to *Yin,* and death. Interestingly Kuan Yin is usually dressed in white.

Hsi Wang Mu was canonized and conscripted into the imperial religion as Niang Niang. But, as the former was already well embedded in the popular mind, Niang Niang remained a largely theological concept distinct from the Goddess who gave her birth. The Goddess of imperial sanction is a sterile version of her predecessor. The Taoist theologians who influenced the Sung Emperors attempted to force the myriad of Gods and ideas into a structure defined by dogma. The result was that they stripped these Gods and myths of their potency, making of them dusty academic entities.

It would be surprising if a Goddess named Mother were not involved in some way with creation. We have seen that one of the Mothers is prayed to by young couples for sons, and that she is particularly prayed to by the barren. Goullart in his fascinating description of the tribal peoples living on the Szechuan-Tibet border describes the festival in honour of an unspecified Niang Niang which took place in the city of Likiang. To the East of the town there is a mountain peak. The worshippers set off at night in order to be on the summit just before sunrise which was the most efficacious time to offer prayers to the Goddess in the temple. "The women prostrated themselves before the Goddess of Niang Niang, the giver of children, and hastily put the bunches of incense and candles before the image. A small priapic God, golden and naked, was touched and kissed by the pious women who so ardently desired children. There he stood in front of the Goddess, like a little boy ready to urinate. Passing this little God, the girls giggled and blushed, averting their faces. Their turn had not yet arrived for such ceremonies." (Peter Goullart: *Forgotten Kingdom*, John Murray, London 1955).

The Jade Emperor

The ancient supreme God was Shang Ti, Superior Emperor, a shadowy, rarely-referred-to figure. He was immensely divorced from the affairs of men. He was the first and everpresent cause of the universe. Such a being had no real relevance to the lives of men. Two processes occurred whose ultimate effect was to bring the Superior Deity closer to man and at the same time become more concrete.

The first of these was the establishment of the Imperial State which necessitated administrative segregation of functions. Life became compartmentalized and an hierarchy was established. The second was the growing importance of Buddhism which had a very complex image of Heaven, Hell and Cycles of Existence. The Taoists, who had taken theological proprietorship of the popular religion, felt threatened. They had to compete at the level of dogma with the Buddhists and bring Heaven into line with the social changes that were taking place around them. As there was no unified Taoist church ideas would vary from area to area, and it was only gradually that some agreement was reached.

Heaven, as an image of society, became a vast bureaucracy with ministries governing every aspect of life possible. There were offices administering thieves, abortions, poisonings, retribution, filial piety, the discovery of treasure, the dispensing of diseases and so on endlessly. There were 36 Heavens, rising upwards in levels of superiority, populated by officials who were Gods. The highest God in the ministries was the God of the Eastern Peak, T'ai Shan. He was the regent over the earth and over man.

To compete with Buddhism, man and his after-life had to be brought into the scheme. This was done simply by saying that all Gods had been men on earth who, because of their virtue, had risen to high rank in the ministries. The world of the mass of the dead is either ignored or placed in a variety of Hells which were taken over completely from the Buddhists. Thus, man and his conduct were brought within the scheme, but without the concept of escape from the miseries of perpetual cycles of existence.

It is this theological structure which has led some to say "Every God, great or small, is a man who after death is promoted... to the dignity of God-head." That is the theory, but, as we have already seen, it is not supported by the facts.

At the head of this bureaucracy is the Jade Emperor — but where is Shang Ti? He has not been wholly left out of the picture, for the Jade Emperor is seen as his successor. In some time in the future he too will hand over to "The Heaven Honoured One of the Dawn of Jade of The Golden Gate". These three beings operate as a supreme triad. This idea too, is stolen from Buddhism which postulates three Buddhas: of the Past, of the Present, and One who is yet to come. The idea of three was also an ancient concept of unity, but the three were seen as everpresent constructs and not defined by the passing of time. Thus, there was T'ai Yi — the underlying unity-joined with Heaven and Earth, and the even more ancient "Tao" and "Te" with their prior yet co-existing nameless cause. The Taoist Pantheon was always headed by a triad, but the members continually changed. The most common, is the idea of the Three Pure Ones, headed by the Jade Emperor, accompanied by Tao Chun — rule of *Yin* and *Yang*, and Lao Tzu.

When the Jade Emperor first appeared is a matter of debate. It appears he may have existed as an idea as early as the ninth century AD, but he only gained his place on the Celestial Throne in 1115 AD, and the story behind this according to Confucian (and therefore suspect) historians, is both amusing and credible. Before telling it, however, we must look at the emperor's position in the State Religion.

The emperor was "Son of Heaven" and ruled by the authority vested in him by Heaven. He was imbued with the virtue of Heaven and this justified his position. Heaven commanded respect and obedience. In this position he had the power to "canonize" men. In theory a God was placed in his position by an act of recognition by the emperor. In practice the emperor recognized those who were already the subjects of popular belief.

Sometimes an emperor could misuse his virtue or the virtue would be weak. In this case, Heaven would manifest its disapproval by disturbing the seasons or causing unnatural events to occur. Drought, floods, earthquakes and the appearance of comets or solar eclipses augered ill. Rebellions would result and it may be that the emperor was deposed, if this happened it was clear that the "Mandate of Heaven" had shifted to the new incumbent for he could not have succeeded without Heaven's blessing.

The Sung Emperor, Chen Tsung, 998–1023, found himself in the unenviable position of facing a real threat to the throne. There had been military defeats and harvests had not been good. In order to preclude revolts which might be successful, he decided to "prove" that he still retained Heaven's mandate. He succumbed to dreams in which he was visited by a God who called himself the Jade Emperor. This event was interpreted in satisfactory fashion by the Imperial sorcerer who is credited with having conceived of the idea in the first place. News of this was published abroad. The emperor heaped titles on this God. In 1015 AD he was made "Highest Author of Heaven, of the Whole Universe, of Human Destinies, of Property, of Rites and the Way, Very August One, Grand Sovereign of Heaven." In 1115 AD he was accorded the only title left: Shang Ti.

He has remained the supreme God ever since. He presides over the councils of Heaven and once a year, on the last day of the year, all the Gods come to his court to hand in their accounts. They are rewarded or punished appropriately.

The Jade Emperor too is caught in the wheel that dictates a prior earthly existence. He is said to have been the son of an ancient emperor, Ch'ing Ti. When he was born a light emanated from him and such was his beauty that none could tear their eyes from looking at him. Incomparable too were his intelligence and compassion. He distributed the funds of the treasury to the sick, the homeless, the halt and the blind. When his father died he succeeded to the throne, but reflecting on the instability of life he retired to a mountain, leaving affairs of state to his ministers. He meditated and on perfecting himself, ascended to Heaven to enjoy perfect eternal life. However, he continually descended to the earth, curing people, teaching universal benevolence and generally assisting the nation and saving the people. Any resemblance between this and the story of Sakyamuni Buddha is of course, wholly coincidental.

Up till now we have referred to him as the Jade Emperor as though it were his name. The Jade aspect is not part of his name, more an attribute of his being. It would be more correct, if more clumsy, to call him The Emperor whose essence is the essence of Jade. He is also sometimes called the Pearly Emperor. The Pearl was thought to have been created through the magical essences of the female principle while Jade is "the most perfect development of the masculine principle in nature." As jade rather than pearl is his prime association, we might conclude that he is more *Yang* than *Yin* but this is not the main reason for attributing to him the essence of jade. Jade is the most precious of stones and symbolizes all that is supremely excellent and most virtuously perfect. Heaven was first represented in the form of a jade disc with a hole in the centre. Later, the emperor, using a disc of this sort, was thought to be able to commune and consult with Heaven. As can be seen from paintings of a later date, all officials had such a disc which they held when in audience with a great Lord. This idea of a disc with a hole in the middle made the bracelet and the ring forms of adornment most natural to jade. Even hanging at the end of a necklace it is usually in this form. Such adornments are not simply worn for aesthetic reasons but ensure safety. Babies and young children often wear a bangle on their arms or legs for this reason. A disc of jade can also be hung in an appropriate spot for *Fung-sui* reasons.

Confucius had this to say about jade: In ancient times men found the likeness of all excellent qualities in jade. Soft, smooth and glossy, it appeared to them like benevolence; fine, compact and strong − like intelligence; angular, but not sharp and cutting − like righteousness; hanging down (in beads) as if it would fall to the ground − like (the humility of) propriety; when struck, yielding a note, clear and prolonged, yet terminating abruptly − like music; its flaws not concealing its beauty, nor its beauty concealing its flaws − like loyalty; with an internal radiance issuing from it on every side − like good faith; bright as a brilliant rainbow − like Heaven; exquisite and mysterious, appearing in hills and streams − like the earth; standing out conspicuously in the symbols of rank − like virtue; esteemed by all under the sky − like the path of truth and duty.

Jade was also one of the materials associated with the elixir of life, capable of giving immortality − or at least extending life for 10,000 years. In later years any concoction professing these properties, whatever its constituents, was called the "Jade Potion".

The Jade Emperor, born of an Imperial hoax, nevertheless found popular approval. Normally represented in the form of a written plaque stating his name, he is here depicted in his Imperial role, holding the, presumably jade, sceptre of his office. An indication of the high respect in which he is held can be seen from a temple in Kaohsiung (Taiwan). The God in the central position is Na Cha, against the back wall, in the position of protection, sits the Buddha but above them both on the next floor is the shrine to Yu Huang Shang Ti − The Jade Emperor.

Pao Kung:
Magistrate Pao

The Chinese love and respect cleverness. In the *Romance of the Three Kingdoms* their favourite hero is not Kuan Yu or Liu Pei but Chuko Liang, affectionately known to all as Kung Ming. He was a strategist, not a warrior hero, and tales of his plots and schemes still delight young and old alike. The kind of cleverness the Chinese enjoy is well illustrated by the following story.

One day a peanut oil-seller went to market to sell his wares. Business was good and he soon sold everything making a tidy sum. As he was picking up to go home a man suddenly came up to him, seized his takings and ran off. The pedlar went to the magistrate and asked for assistance but was told that, as there was no evidence of any sort, there was little that could be done.

Soon afterwards, the magistrate, who was well known for his sagacity and highly respected for his honesty and impartiality, caused posters to be put up all over town advertising the judgement of the stone. Anyone who wished to observe the proceedings was welcome to come on payment of a few cents.

Such a curious event was bound to be highly popular and the whole town turned up to witness the occasion. At the entrance to the hall there was a large pot of water and the people were invited to drop their money in the water. At the bottom of the pot was the stone. The culprit was among the crowd and when his turn came he too dropped a coin into the water. The coin sank to the bottom and hit the rock causing bubbles of oil to surface. The man was immediately arrested. The stone had judged.

The magistrate of this story was Magistrate Pao, of whom there are a great many such stories. He was a real person who achieved some eminence in the Sung Dynasty. His dates are 999–1062. This was a time of relative peace and prosperity. Forty years before his birth, there had been a civil war that had decimated the population of China from 53 million to 17 million. Sixty years after his death the Kin Tribe from the North occupied the whole of China, north of the Yangtze River. They were to remain there for another hundred years. In between these events no great catastrophes seem to have occurred. Such times allow individuals to put self before state and it appears that villainy and corruption were rife. Pao Ch'eng, as a magistrate, was well placed to line his pocket but he did not do so. He stood out as an honest man and an impartial administrator of the law.

Pao Ch'eng was a magistrate in the Sung capital, present-day K'aifeng. Before this he had probably been a provincial magistrate who through ability had come to Imperial notice and been promoted to the capital. However, the abilities that brought about his promotion led eventually to his downfall. He was accused of nepotism and transferred away from the capital. History of the popular kind has absolved him and laid the blame for his demotion on the machinations of enemies. He was later promoted to the higher office of Vice-Minister of Ceremony, where no doubt he was rendered ineffective. The pattern of this career was by no means uncommon. The temporary absence of officials from the capital being, on occasion, politic as the emperor did a balancing act between the vying factions at court.

The charge of nepotism and the fact that the Imperial Censor at that time was one Pao Lao-yeh who, similarly, had a reputation for being that the reputation of the one has been added to the other and the acts of the magistrate attributed to the censor. I refer to a curious story quoted by Burkhardt relating to Pao Lao-yeh.

One Tsao Ching-chih, brother-in-law to the emperor and brother of one of the eight immortals, fell in love with an attractive lady who was, unfortunately married. He killed the husband, and, when the lady refused to give in to his advances, locked her up in a dungeon. News of this came to Pao Lao-yeh through the appearance of the spirit of the murdered husband. He began to investigate the case. Tsao panicked and tried to murder the woman but she was saved by a star God and managed to escape.

Running down the road she saw a procession and, thinking it was the Imperial Censor's, she stopped it and presented her complaint. Unfortunately the man she was addressing was Tsao's elder brother, the future immortal. On the pretext that she had behaved disrespectfully, he ordered that she be beaten to death. Evidently a tough lady, she survived and made her way to see Pao Lao-yeh. The brothers were tried and condemned to death. The younger brother, despite entreaties from the emperor, was executed. To save the elder, the emperor declared an amnesty, and he, knowing the wrong he had done, went to a hermitage and spent the rest of his life in meditation.

This story is interesting in that it assumes that the lady would naturally go to see the Imperial Censor and that he himself would prosecute the case. The Imperial Censor was one of the most senior members of government and his duties were to report all irregularities and wrongs, offer advice to the emperor and above all to criticize the emperor. The irregularities and wrongs were those occurring in the conduct of government by ministers and governors. Criminal cases such as this one would have been referred to a magistrate.

The Board of Justice did not come under the Censorate but under the State Affairs department. For this reason it is very unlikely that the Imperial Censor would have conducted the case personally. The story is however, very similar to some told of Pao Ch'eng in which it is a supernatural visitation rather than his own cleverness which exposes the culprit.

In Chinese folklore the magistrate is commonly portrayed as grasping, oppressive and corrupt. To see why this is so it is worth describing the nature of the position, its possibilities and its dangers.

Magistrates obtained their positions through success in the state exams. These exams tested scholars on their knowledge of the Confucian classics. On passing these exams, and at certain periods in Chinese history monetary gifts were necessary to attain this, scholars would be appointed to a position in the civil service. The magistrate was the lowest rung in the hierarchy.

Schooling in the classics would certainly have encouraged the development of the ability to analyse problems as well as instilling orthodoxy. But it can have done little to prepare the future magistrate in the ways of men or in fiscal management. This first posting made and unmade men.

Magistrates were posted to a county where they were the most senior official – and therefore, in theory, held most power. Their job was to administer their district, collect taxes, assess families, register land, maintain horses and staging posts, repair roads and, of course, decide in cases of dispute and bring criminals to justice.

Clearly one man could not do this and so many of his responsibilities had to be delegated. If harvests were good, imperial demands light, taxes fair, local aristocrats, landowners and tax collectors honest and the magistrate seen to be impartial then clearly there would be few problems. Such a blissful state of affairs would have been extremely rare. Not only did the magistrate have to contend with natural disasters which would in turn affect the taxes collected — out of which he himself was paid — but vested interests on all sides often served to compound his problems.

Usually maligned, most magistrates were in fact honest Confucians who attempted to do their best in near impossible conditions. One such was Huang Liu-hung who arrived in T'an Ch'eng county in Shantung province in 1670. This area had been devastated by bandits and rebels for fifty years. Floods had reduced the usable land by half and two years before an earthquake had destroyed their houses and not a single grain was harvested that year. Half the people were dying of starvation. The processes of government were slow which meant that tax demands and labour requirements were fixed at impossibly high levels — and it took constant pressing to obtain reductions. In this case taxes had not been collected for thirteen years. In the year after his arrival there was a plague of locusts. Despair was endemic and the extent of it can be seen from the fact that one of Huang's first edicts was aimed at reducing the number of suicides. While conditions in T'an Ch'eng must have been exceptionally bad there can have been few places which did not, at one time or another, suffer from natural and social disruption of some severity.

Although in theory the magistrate was all-powerful in his domain, in practice, large landowners, local gangs, guilds and lords would be able to manipulate the law. If he was not careful he could be broken by these interests. If he made too many demands on the populace they would rebel. If lawlessness and partiality were too evident, word would reach the Governor to whom the magistrate was directly responsible. The job involved a very careful balancing act at the best of times.

In the case of crimes, suspects had to confess before they could be sentenced. In order to obtain confessions, torture was sanctioned and widely used. Even Magistrate Pao was not averse to using these means to attain his ends.

Tortures used included beatings, the wearing of a cangue — a wooden portable pillary borne on the shoulders — and finger and ankle screws. These were sanctioned by the penal code but other forms of torture, though illegal, were used. These included flogging with whips of hooks, the wearing of iron shirts and various forms of burning or scalding.

Torture was not the only means of extracting confessions. Psychological tricks were also used, often involving the suggestion that Heaven had interceded and informed the magistrate of the true state of affairs. Among superstitious people this would have had great effect.

Just as the emperor was judged by the stars and the elements so too was the magistrate. He too had his diffused portion of the Heavenly Mandate. This mandate depended on the submission of people to his power and their respect for his authority. If the people had no respect, or, if life was too unbearable, they would find means of discomfiting the magistrate. The people have always had the power of being obstinate, intransigent and unobliging. If the magistrate could not coerce or persuade the people to obey his edicts he would not be able to fulfil his obligations to the Central Government. If there was unrest the Governor of the region would hear of it and intervene. The life of a magistrate was no sinecure.

All governments rely on the acquiescence of the populace to their rule. There must at least be a minimal consensus of opinion that there are benefits to be gained from serving the state. If the people are to have even a nominal faith in the state, the possibility of justice at the hands of its agents has to exist. By deifying Magistrate Pao the people expressed their faith in this possibility as well as their contempt for the corrupt biased official of popular conception.

The first stories relating to him appeared 150 years after his death and appear to have been based on fact. Whether they were written in response to popular belief or were themselves the source of his reputation it is hard to say. By the thirteenth century, oral and highly fictionalized accounts had begun to appear and many of these were later committed to paper in the Ming Dynasty.

In the illustration he is represented as an official, his dark face, a symbol of impartiality, holding the wooden sceptre of his position. On either side are his attendants, one holding his seal of office and the other, wide-eyed, with a rod of punishment. The contrast of yellow and purple indicate his importance in bringing about imperial stability. What appears to be a bowl of fruit around his navel is a design on his robes and possibly similar in effect to the insignia that our armed forces call "spaghetti". The character on the seal is his imperial commission.

Hung Sheng:
Hung — The Holy One

It is often a salutary corrective to enter a temple and enquire about the deities enshrined there. These temples are run by old men or women who have the privilege of keeping them and who make their living from donations. These keepers are not expected to be theological experts, nevertheless one feels they might have picked up some of the story or stories of the Gods they guard.

I went to two temples dedicated to Hung Sheng, both times with a friend to do the interpreting and both times I returned empty-handed. The keepers knew nothing at all. The second time, when pressed, the old lady stated that he was like Kuan Yin.

Any account of Chinese religion must take into consideration this incurious acceptance of divinities. They are, they have their specializations and they are to be worshipped. All else is superfluous.

One man told me emphatically that he was Tin Hau's brother but that was the end of his knowledge.

Do we then know anything about Hung Sheng? Very little, I'm afraid. Burkhardt encountered the same problems and came up with a more colourful biography. Hung Sheng, he was told by one informant, was the re-incarnation of the Sea Dragon of the Southern Seas. Another version is that he was one Hung Hsi, an official of the T'ang Dynasty who during his tenure encouraged the study of mathematics, astronomy and geography and who established an observatory whose weather predictions were of great help to fishermen. He died young on the thirteenth day of the second moon of an unspecified year and the emperor, on being memorialized, that is to say, petitioned, declared him worthy of worship.

There is something too cut and dried about this story to be wholly acceptable. The emperor wouldn't canonize him before he was actually being worshipped and, as we saw in the Tin Hau legend, it takes a while for the people who knew the person to come to terms with the new status. A prophet is not recognized in his own country.

Nevertheless, it appears he may have been canonized though at what date we do not know. He has a title but this may be of local rather than imperial origin. It would seem that his connection with Tin Hau is not enshrined in any myth but is simply a way of stating that they are both sea divinities. His association with Kuan Yin probably derives from the fact that they both have overlordship of the Southern Ocean. Is this why he has the yellow halo of Bodhisattva-hood?

On canonization he was given the title Holy Great King Hung of Kuang Li and Nan Hai. These sound like names of places but can be translated as "Hall of (or enlarged) profit" and "Southern Ocean". Now if we are to take these literally the "hall of profit" would relate to the North and this may have been included in the title to counteract the negative aspect of the South which is associated with doors and therefore bad luck. The fact that Hung Sheng is given overlordship of the Southern Ocean is a fairly clear statement of his origins for traditionally the oceans were ruled over by the Sea Dragons. The idea that he is a personification of this mythical animal gains strength when we realize that Hung, while being a surname, also means flood.

The Dragon rules over the eastern quadrant, but is also the animal emblem of the fifth month which relates to the hall of summer. It is said that in spring it ascends to the Heavens and in autumn it buries itself in the water, thus it announces the cyclical changes of the seasons. In some respects it embodies the forces of the universe. Each quarter has a dragon who keeps vigilance over the affairs of that season. The dragon is thus a benevolent being. Dragon lore of later origin posits three different types of dragon: the Lung who are in heaven, the Li who are in the sea and the Chiao who resides in marshes and mountains. We see that dragon myths posit first one whose cycle of existence relates to the seasons, then four governing the quadrants, then hundreds. We cannot reconcile them within one system.

The concept of the dragon seems to have originated in the South though it had spread to the rest of China long before the country became unified. Since the founding of the Han Dynasty (202 BC) the dragon has been the emblem of imperial power. The main dragon festival, a festival largely confined to the South, is the Dragon Boat Festival. On the fifth day of the fifth month fishing communities along the coast conduct races in long slim boats which have the heads and tails of dragons. In the centre there is a drum which is beaten to provide a rhythm for the rowers. At some predetermined spot the rowers throw in packets of glutinous rice wrapped in leaves. The story tells that this event commemorates the death of one Ch'u Yuan, a statesman who, in 296 BC, in protest against the corruption of government threw himself into the river Mi-lo. The people, who loved him for his virtue, sent out boats and tried to deflect the fish from his body but it was never found. This story is internally suspect for he is supposed to be far from his home state when he threw himself into the river and therefore presumably a stranger to the people of the area. Ch'u Yuan literally means "forgive grievances" and it is more than likely this was, if not the name of the offerings, at least the intention behind them. The true origin of this rite lies in the desire to placate the sea dragons with food offerings made from the first grain of the year. The fifth day of the fifth month being the most suitable as five, the central number of the magic square, is the number attributed to the dragon. He is the fifth of the animals designating the years. At this time, though, perhaps not on this day, similar offerings were made to the ancestors, to the mountains and the rivers. The object of these offerings was to ensure that the Gods continued to be benign.

Hung Sheng "died" on the thirteenth day of the second moon. This is two days before the spring equinox, the time when the dragon leaves the waters and ascends to the Heavens. He is prayed to for clement conditions at sea. Whether he suffers the same indignities as Lung Wang, the Dragon King, is an open question, for should the Dragon Boat Festival fail to produce the rain necessary for the crops the image of this deity is exposed to the sun to sweat. Hung Sheng is the personification of the Dragon King but this deity survives in his own form and has charge over the Eastern Ocean.

Tsai Shen:
God of Wealth

From the earliest records we hear of autumn as a time of feasting, and of giving, it was a time of extravagant generosity. Only thus could one's prosperity be recognized. Since all gave in excess of what had been given all were enriched by mutual esteem. Wealth should not be hoarded – that was the first principle.

As peasant villages grew into towns and as the kingdoms gave way to Empire, this extravagance took on different forms but remained essential. Wealth and its distribution or destruction was and is the pre-requisite of importance and respect.

Today, after dinner in a restaurant there is often a long argument over who should pay the bill, each man insisting on it. It is an exercise in controversy that puts the European at a grave disadvantage. The idea of each man paying his share is inconceivable. Again, gambling is a passion. Games of mahjong are taken very seriously – so seriously that a number of prohibitions have grown up. One must never, for example, enter a room in which this game is being played, carrying a book. The words for "book" and "to lose" have the same sound. At these apparently social games relatively large amounts of money are won or lost. In one hour over a game of cards a man, who may only earn $1,000 a month, may lose $50 – and this over a casual game.

In business too, the Chinese display a very different approach. In Britain we tend to be very conservative when it comes to investing our money. We place great emphasis on security. A Chinese family is always on the look out for a good proposition and will think nothing of putting ten years of savings into a venture such as a shop or restaurant. Should the business collapse it is a tragedy but the memory of it will not deter them from doing exactly the same ten years later. I was told of a businessman who had amassed $10 million. He decided to make it work for him. He put $1 million into ten different projects knowing that maybe half would fail and only a few make a profit. He hoped that one would prove to be immensely profitable and more than make up for his losses. We see that high risks do not, as they would in the West, invalidate a proposition.

If a man has had some good luck, or he has made a good deal or he is opening a shop, he will give a large banquet to celebrate the fact. Guests will often bring a red packet of "lucky money" and hand it over when they sign their name on the red scroll which will be kept to commemorate the event. This too is the procedure at weddings. The sum collected in this manner is expected to cover the expenses of the dinner.

When a lion dance is performed outside a shop — the lion symbolizing protection — a red packet is in evidence. Often it is placed in an awkward position and it is part of the object of the dance to see how dexterously the lion is able to extract it. I once saw a lion having problems getting at an envelope placed on a dish under a tin bowl all supported by chopsticks set out in the shape of a crab. Often the red packet is tied to a sprig of Chinese cabbage. This is a pun on the sound *Choi* meaning cabbage and money, though the tones are different.

It is at New Year that lucky money is most widely distributed. One does not merely give a verbal wish for prosperity but gives money itself. This largesse is not distributed by everybody indiscriminately. There are rules. The prime rule is that the married give to the unmarried though there are amendments to the clause i.e. employers to employees and old to young.

Recently one young boy was asked on radio how much he expected to get in "laissee" at Chinese New Year. $100,000 was his reply. He was, he explained, from quite a wealthy family.

The red packet, itself, has on it, in gold, a design which will often include the following: the character we call double happiness (囍) for marital bliss — a condition dependent on the wife producing sons; a peach and/or pine denoting longevity and a fish for success in business or studies. Wealth does not simply refer to money. Money is only one portion of a composite idea. Long life and male descendants are also wealth in a very real sense.

We see this in the picture of the God. The mandarin God has a ring of cash around the hem of his gown, on his breast is the motif of a lotus (fertility) and in his hand is a golden mushroom (longevity). One of his acolytes is carrying deer horn (potency) and the other a bowl of cash and what seems to be golden grass. It may be that this is exactly what it is, for there is a theory that the character for 10,000 denotes the number of grass in a field and that grass is for that reason symbol of 10,000. The number 10,000 itself has the implication of absolute number as in the cries to the Emperor "May you live 10,000 years". "May you have 10,000 sons" etc. The mushroom, or it may be a lotus – depending on the tradition one follows, was the plant on which a sceptre was modelled. This sceptre was carried by officials and was often made of jade. Called a *Ju I* sceptre, it seems to have derived from a short sword and may be connected with an ancient phallic cult. The Buddhists see it as a symbol of destruction and conquest. Our mandarin God is holding such a sceptre. His gown is pink in colour and it seems this is a colour associated with *Yin*, peach blossom, spring and the moon. In Mandarin only a tone difference separates the sound of the world for silver and the quality *Yin.* All metal is *Yin.*

The Chinese, following the rule of fives, posit five happinesses: Old Age, High Rank, Wealth, Sons, Pleasure. As three is the number of plurality – the five have become three. One sees them everywhere, the God of Longevity with his high-domed head, the God of High Rank who holds the sceptre of authority and the God of Happiness who stands a head taller than the others and who is always placed at the centre. They go together as *Fu'k, Lu'k, Sao* – In Mandarin, *Fu, Lu, Shou.* Here, happiness, *Fu'k,* includes wealth and sons, for these are the basics and this explains his pre-eminence.

Just as *Fu'k* literally means happiness and is therefore the God of Happiness so Ts'ai Shen means the God of Wealth. Money is important therefore there is, of necessity, a God who oversees the heavenly directorate governing its acquisition, the amounts to be allotted etc. Or so the theory goes. In fact there are several Gods of Wealth.

Kuan Ti is patron of pawn shops and sudden windfalls – a curious combination reflecting, perhaps, the dual financial implications entailed in the sacking of a city by an army: poverty, and therefore good business for pawn shops, for the people; sudden wealth for the army. Although Kuan Ti is a military God, his most noteworthy characteristic is his insistence on right conduct. This sits rather uneasily with such patronage. Popular instinct, however, can't be wrong. There is another reason why Kuan Ti is connected with wealth – or so I will argue. Before doing so I will have to return to Ts'ai Shen.

Ts'ai Shen, worshipped under the respectful name Ts'ai Shen Yeh – grandfather – in family shrines, is also worshipped under the name Lu Hsing, the Star God of High Rank. Burkhardt names two mortal candidates who are supposed to have risen to this position. One of them is Ch'ao Kung Ming a hermit from Szechuan who was called to Heaven to wage war on the side of "The High Priest of Taoism" (?). He was successful. His opponents however, built an image of him out of straw, made incantations to the image for 49 days then shot it through the heart with arrows made of peach wood. He died immediately. This story is also told of Kuan Ti.

Ch'ao Kung-ming rode a black tiger, used pearls as hand grenades, wielded a steel whip and is often depicted with a black face. He is also shown carrying ingots — as he is here but without his other trappings. Here he almost looks like a Chinese Santa Claus. Only his blue cloak retains the connection with things dark and thus, inevitably, with the North. On his deification he was given the title Hsuan T'an Shang Ti.

The Hsuan T'an, the "dark altar" — is in the centre of the temple. It's position is indicated by the prayer stool in front of the altar — it can also refer to the entire area from the centre to the main altar but not including the shrines on each side. He is therefore the supreme ruler of the place of prayer.

Another contender for the post is a sage called Pi Kan who was, according to legend, related ,to the infamous, last emperor of the Shang Dynasty. Pi Kan berated the emperor on his wickedness, upon which he was ordered to undergo an operation to see if his heart had seven (sacred number for Buddhists) orifices. Pi Kan did not recover.

Pi Kan (比干) may have been a man but, on the grounds that anything attributed to the end of the Shang Dynasty is suspect, we can probe further. "Pi" means to compare, "Kan" can be a surname. The other meaning of "Kan" — arms, crime — do not seem to be very helpful. But "Kan" is also used in combination with other characters to crete meaning and the most common is Chu Kan (竹干), bamboo. Chinese use of language favours abbreviation and it is not unlikely that Pi Kan means "compare bamboo". This makes sense.

In order to divine your fortune you can go to a temple and, while in a position of obeisance to the God, shake a large bamboo holder containing bamboo slips. When one slip has fallen, the number on it is given to the temple keeper who will give you a slip of paper. The characters need to be interpreted. Pi Kan, if my theory is correct, is the spirit overseeing this activity.

Pi Kan and Hsuan T'an Shang Ti are not conflicting proponents for one position. Both have their place as is evident by the fact that they are often depicted together under the guises of Civil and Military Gods of Wealth. They complement each other. One guards the place of worship, the other influences the way the bamboo falls. Fortune relates primarily to wealth.

Bamboo is also associated with war which was known, in previous times, as Kan Wo (干戈), bamboo (and) weapons. Arrows, were fired into the air at times of eclipse and contain the idea of restoring fortune; bamboo is a symbol of longevity. It is at least likely that this connection of war with good fortune and long life necessitated, by associational logic, the inclusion of Kuan Ti as a God of Wealth.

While some worshippers will visit a temple simply to pay their respects, it is more common that they will go to ask for help or to assess their fortune. Good fortune is primarily related to wealth — it is more than apt that the Gods of Wealth are inextricably involved in the process of prayer. All prayer takes place under the aegis of the God of Wealth and one's fortune is in his hands. Pray hard.

The Peach Blossom Girl:
T'ao Hua Hsien Nii

There was nothing more infuriating in my investigation than to ask
about a God, to find that everybody recognizes the name but no more.
So it was with the Peach Blossom Girl. I was finally fortunate enough
to find a comfortably plump, middle-aged lady who was happy, for a
short while, to tell me a story. It went like this:—

To Fa Lui (as she is called in Cantonese) was formed from the
sword and the God of Wealth, Chao Kung, from the scabbard of
Pak Tai. This Chao Kung was a fortune-teller, One day a woman
came to him to ask her son's fortune and he told her that her son
would die that night. The woman was in despair, To Fa Lui heard
her crying and asked her what the matter was — she then told the
woman how to save him. The woman was to keep calling out her
son's name. The son, who was far away, heard her and rushed out
of a hut. As soon as he was outside, the hut collapsed to the
ground. The next day they both went back to Chao Kung and
demanded her money back. They also broke his shop sign into
pieces — so destroying his reputation. The son's name was Pa Yee.
Some time later he went back to Chao Kung to have his fortune
told and Chao Kung told him he would die in three years. Son
and mother went to To Fa Lui who told them to make some flour
peaches for the God of Longevity. She then told him where to
find him. The son went off with his present and found two old
men playing chess. He offered them his peaches and at the end of
the game he told them of his problem. In return for his present
they each gave him 400 years, so giving him a life span of 818
years.

The last part of this story is familiar and keeps recurring in different
contexts though the number of years allotted varies. Here there is a clear
association of sounds. There is only a tone difference between the

word for four and the word for death. The flour peaches that the son presents are a very rich symbol of long life.

Peaches are emblematic of marriage, immortality and spring. The God of Longevity is often pictured as emerging from a peach and in the garden of the Queen of Western Heaven there is a peach garden, the peaches of which are the fruits of eternal life. The symbolism of flour is not so obvious until the character is broken down — giving us "honour of wheat"; the word for wheat however, is closely associated with that for the pulse, the line of succession and parentage.

No story is complete without these symbolic touches but far more fundamental to this tale is the opposition of To Fa Lui and Chao Kung. If people remember anything, it is this. Chao Kung, as we saw in the last chapter is one of the Gods of Wealth and is often called "bright general Chao".

This conflict is echoed in another episode in which she kills him by making an effigy of him and piercing it with arrows made of peach wood; he was immune to the steel of her sword.

How are we to make sense of the fact that a clearly benevolent young lady kills one of the Gods of Wealth? The answer is complex and we must take our time to unravel it slowly.

The Peach Blossom Girl is the fairy spirit of that flower. Each month has its flower emblem and the peach flower is emblem of the second month, which lies in the hall of spring (see magic square). However it is at the time of the New Year that it bursts into blossom. On the night before the New Year the flower markets and nurseries are packed with families who are looking for sprigs of the peach tree. It is important that they make the right choice for it must not blossom until it is within the house. It should then blossom within the first three days. If it does, this is a portent of wealth and good fortune. At this time of the year a spray of blossom is placed at the door and this prevents the entrance of evil.

The connection of the Peach Blossom Girl with marriage is appropriate as spring has always been considered the most propitious season for this event. Her image will be bought by a mother for the protection of the bride. As here, in our illustration, she is shown in the militaristic costume familiar to anyone who has seen Chinese opera. From her back four flags stick out. Each flag represents an army. Her flags are black (north) and bear the character 福 , invoking happiness. She is brandishing a sword by the scabbard end.

A scabbard is, I think, a more fitting symbol of the female, while a sword relates more obviously to the male – T'ao meaning scabbard is closer in sound to T'ao meaning peach than is Tao meaning sword. The statue of the Peach Blossom Girl in the temple of Jade Vacuity on Cheung Chau also shows her holding the scabbard, not the sword, which is nevertheless present in both cases. If she is to act as a protector against evil spirits she must wield a sword – the essential weapon of all exorcists. Our only solution is to assume that, at different levels of meaning, she is associated with both sword and scabbard.

The entry of a girl into her new family entails symbolic danger. We remember the importance of the doorway and the need for protection. All who enter on their own volition are potential threats. Marriage involves the permanent entry of an unknown quality. If the bride came in voluntarily there would be danger. For this reason the traditional ceremony involves the token capture and kidnapping of the bride. She becomes plunder and is thus an addition to the wealth of the bridegroom's family. She also represents wealth in a much more basic way for it is through her that the family line will continue.

The lot of a wife in her new home was and still is often a hard one. She lived under her mother-in-law's thumb all the time. Her sole importance lay in producing sons. Women will worship the God of the Soil for sons, in spring, and at other times they will pray to Kuan Yin. The Peach Blossom Girl brandishing her sheathed sword exorcises all demons that stand in the way of the marital sheathing of swords.

For a wife, and thus for the sons that she will bear, the bridegroom's family have to pay a sum of money. The amount to be paid is, of course, subject to bargaining but will be substantial; $10,000 would be considered cheap today. For the undisposable wealth of the future, the disposable wealth of the present is needed. The cost of a marriage involves not only this payment, but also the cost of the wedding dinner and of gifts of food that have to be presented. It is an expensive business.

That the spirit of the God of the Bride should kill the image of the God of Wealth is simply an appropriate expression of the facts of life.

The Pak Tai connection is interesting especially when we remember that Chao Kung is the God of the Dark Altar. This altar is that area in which one prays. One never offers abstract prayers – one prays for something. The dark altar is the place where one "compares bamboo" – where one seeks omens. The original method of divination was with the bones of ancestors and the Shamans united with the spirits of the dead before making their prophecies.

In the story at the beginning of this chapter Chao Kung was a fortune teller whose predictions were twice foiled by T'ao Hua Hsien Nii. Interesting, because the character for peach tree breaks down into "tree of omens" and when "omen" is connected to "earth" it refers to the border of the grave. Fate is separate from the prediction. The prediction may be sound but the fate can be avoided. A change in one's fate destroys the validity of the prediction and thus of the fortune-teller. The peach tree is clearly associated with "good omens". I wonder if the peach tree was once worshipped purely to avert evil. I have read no mention of such worship, yet the wood of the peach tree is necessary for the art of exorcism.

Knowledge of the future is connected with the dead. Divination is under the aegis of the two Gods of Wealth. Pak Tai's association with wealth and good fortune is inevitable.

Chang Hsien:
The Immortal Chang

Of all the pictures in my collection this is my favourite. It has a simple, human charm which the others lack. The immortal Chang is shown preparing to fire an arrow at the Celestial Dog while two boys clutch his gown.

One story of this God's origin is equally delightful for it is based on a deceit. The King of Shu (Szechuan) was defeated and killed by Sung T'ai Tsu, founder of the Sung Dynasty. The King of Shu's wife was taken into Sung T'ai Tsu's harem as a concubine. He must have been very taken with her for he would drop in on her quarters from time to time. On one occasion, he entered her rooms to find her kneeling before the picture of her dead husband, a most virtuous action in the Chinese eyes. The emperor demanded to know who the man was and, fearing to tell the truth, she told him it was one of the Gods of her region: the Immortal Chang who gives children.

It is possible that this story was told not to describe the derivation of the God but simply as an amusing anecdote in connection with him. His origins can be traced back to the first century AD when his person was connected with a cult in Szechuan. This cult can be traced further back to an ancient custom at one time common throughout China but surviving longest in that region which remained an outpost of Chinese civilization. When a boy was born a bow made of mulberry wood was hung on the left of the door. When the child was accepted by the head of the family, the bow was taken down and used to fire six arrows. One into the sky, one into the earth and one in the direction of each of the cardinal points of the compass. The object of this was to ward off evil. In the Szechuan dialect the phrase "to bend a bow" sounds like "Mr. Chang". Some say we owe to this association of sounds the personification of an agrarian custom. The name Chang itself, breaks down into "to draw a bow".

The use of mulberry wood is purely emblematic, no magical properties are imputed to this plant. Mulberry, the leaves of which feed the silk worms, symbolizes industry and homely comforts. In the belief that this plant only grew in China it also represented the native soil, and as earth is *Yin* so a branch of the mulberry was carried when mourning a mother while bamboo was carried for a father. Together these two plants are symbols of filial piety.

There was also a myth that the sun emerged from a mulberry tree which may be a metaphorical expression of the idea that *Yin* (mulberry tree — earth) brought forth *Yang* (the sun).

As China developed the mechanisms of state, the centre moved gradually east. In the west, Szechuan remained on the fringe of events. Its craggy mountains drew the hermits, its fertile plains ensured its prosperity. Because it changed more slowly it remained the repository of agrarian tradition. This tradition finds another echo in the Immortal Chang.

In the Feudal period the lord was the focus of virtue and universal unity. The order of the universe manifested itself in the regularity of life. The regular had to be constantly invoked. If the acts appropriate to the season were left undone then heaven was thrown off-course: rain fell when it should be dry, it was hot when it should be cold. When the sun and moon had lost their way there was an eclipse. This was disaster. The brunt of this fell on the Lord. It was for him to maintain order and regulate the seasons. If there was an eclipse he had to take action to put heaven back on its proper course.

To do this he put everybody on a war footing. The men of the east wore green, of the north, black, of the west, white, of the south, red, and the retainers of the Lord at the centre wore yellow. They were set in a square, the Lord struck a great drum and the vassals fired arrows at the area of darkness. Only when social order was perfectly organized could the heavens follow suit and the order of nature be re-established.

Even though eclipses were capable of being predicted as early as eighth century BC they were still connected with disaster and people still go out of doors with pots and pans and bang them together until all is well again. A story grew up quite early on that eclipses were caused by a celestial dog who periodically attempts to swallow the moon but is frightened away by the noise and the arrows.

There is a conjunction here with an Indian legend which believes that a solar eclipse occurs when the Sun God is swallowed by a demon. A recent solar eclipse caused a policeman in the town of Ahmedabad to shoot ten rounds into the sky because he was hurt by the "invasion of the moon of the sun". The report stated that he went "berserk" but, apart from his emotional state, his actions followed traditional dictates.

There is a story that the Sung Emperor Jen Tsung dreamt one night of a handsome young man whose skin was white and whose hair was pitch black. He carried a bow. The man told the emperor that the star T'ien Kou (the Heavenly Dog) was in the sky threatening the earth and moon while on earth it would devour little children. Only his presence kept the dog at bay. The emperor awoke and ordered a portrait of the boy to be painted and displayed in public.

It seems clear from the number of references to the emperors of the Sung that Chang Hsien was something of a patron of theirs, and that this fact encouraged popular worship and myth making. The Sung Emperors are commonly believed to have been only half Chinese. They are referred to as "Northerners", and probably had foreign blood. The importance of this will be seen later.

The Celestial Dog, is not always feared or despised. His master is Erh Lang, whose name literally means "number two chap" and who is The Jade Emperor's nephew — we don't know who his father is. Erh Lang is credited with being a magician and it was he who finally effected the capture of Monkey. There are many stories of Erh Lang and the Heavenly Hound, though Erh Lang is usually outshone by his pet. One of the stories goes like this:—

There was a Goddess of the mountain Wah Shan whose name was Shing Mo. Shing Mo fell in love with a mortal and they married and had a son whom they called Chan Heung (a type of fragrant wood). The Jade Emperor was greatly displeased with her conduct and demanded that she return to Heaven. She refused so he sent Erh Lang and Tien Kou (the Celestial Dog) to bring her back. Their arrival at Wah Shan was marked by a ferocious thunderstorm and lightning crackled in the sky. As with all such battles, each participant has a bagful of tricks and transformations. However, after a fearful battle Shing Mo was captured and, as punishment for her action, locked into the mountain with the Emperor's seal. (This is identical to the story of Monkey's capture).

As the years passed her husband took another wife and had another son by her. Both sons went to the capital and there, the first son came out top in the examinations. Before taking up a post, he begged leave to go home.

As he neared his home, he heard a loud wailing and on asking who was there, he discovered it was his mother. This was the first he knew of it for his father had never told him the truth. When he was at last convinced and had recovered from his shock, he asked her if he could do anything to set her free. She told him there was nothing he could do. However, Shing Mo's maid, Ling-chi, appeared to the son and gave him a magic axe, telling him that with this he could break the seal. He thereupon broke the seal and freed his mother. Great was the joy of their re-uniting.

The joy was shortlived for news soon arrived that the younger brother had accidentally hurt the First Minister's son and was threatened with being executed. Although he was not her son, Shing Mo wielded her magic powers and he was saved. Shing Mo now returned to her husband and his other wife and they lived happily ever after.

This story is not altogether very interesting and appears to have been patched together from other stories. It does, however, illustrate very well that Erh Lang and T'ien Kou are really nothing more than Heaven's bully boys.

Erh Lang and the Celestial Dog had a temple in Peking. If it is still there — it was twenty years ago — it is the oldest temple extant. It commemorates their saving Peking from being inundated with water. When the emperor went to pray to the sun he avoided passing it.

As the dog is one of the animals of the calendar and his influence operates between 7 p.m. and 9 p.m., women who are born at this time or in this year are in danger of having their children stolen. It is therefore important that they take steps to prevent this from happening. They will hang an image of Chang Hsien over their beds. He is the patron of pregnant women and he can also be prayed to for offspring. This aspect was especially common in the Sung Dynasty when childless families would pray to a tablet on which his name had been written. As we shall see, Chang Hsien does not confine his protective influences to pregnancy and birth. He is also responsible for ensuring that succeeding generations revere their predecessors in the chain of life.

As if to mirror the image of Chang Hsien firing arrows at the dog one can also find pictures in every way identical except that the dog is replaced by a rat and the bow is arrowless.

In certain respects the Chinese see similarities between dogs and rats. Both are connected with death; the dog because of its connection with the eclipse and the rat through its association with north. Both are also connected with wealth — a stray dog attaching itself to the home and the arrival of a large rat with a distended stomach are both taken as signs of imminent riches. Conversely the arrival of a cat portends poverty. This is not to say that rats are particularly welcomed. Their destructive capacity is well-recognized. As dogs are eaten so are rats and I feel sure that the digestion of these animals has symbolic virtue in much the same way that cannibals don't eat people because they have a taste for human flesh but rather to incorporate into themselves the power of their enemies.

Interestingly the rat, which also symbolizes timidity, meanness and industry was thought to change into a quail in the spring. The quail is an emblem of courage and of poverty.

By drawing an empty bow at a rat Chang Hsien is invoking wealth for the children.

It should be made clear that Chang Hsien's protection applies only to male children. Until very recently the Chinese word for children applied primarily to sons. If a man was asked how many children he had he would only count the boys. A man with no "children" might yet have several daughters. This concern with sons is given recognition on the symbolic level. Chang Hsien is Heaven's *maitre d'*. He presides over the culinary department of the Gods and is in charge of ordering the banquets.

As we saw in the introduction, ancestor worship imposed on the sons of the family the "burden" of honouring the entire ancestral line — itself composed primarily of males. They did this by taking care of the graves of their immediate fathers and mothers as well as by paying their respects to ancestral tablets in the home. Food is always present and naturally is offered to the most senior first, that is to say to the dead. When they have extracted the essence of the food the living can partake of their portion. The well-being of the dead depends on the living to supply them with their needs. In return the well-being of the living depends on how well they treat their ancestors who have it in their power to punish or reward. Those of the dead who were sufficiently vigorous in life to produce many sons could expect to be well fed in Heaven. Those who, for whatever misfortune, had no sons to worship them were consigned to a spiritual existence far from the banquet halls of Heaven. These spirits are called the "hungry" ghosts.

Burkhardt has this to say of the hungry ghosts. "The Chinese believe that the spirits of those bereft of the consolations of ancestral worship are malignant, and may claim living substitutes, unless they are pacified by food." Each year they are released from Heaven for a period of two weeks starting on the fifteenth day of the seventh month. In rural areas these two weeks are a time for making food offerings and burning paper talismans. It is no coincidence that the fifteenth is also the first day on which moon cakes are sold in preparation for the Autumn Moon festival. This is the harvest celebration. The month prior to the final gathering in of the harvest is a time of maximum danger to the entire community. Ghosts whose own descendants are no longer represented among the living can feel no responsibility for the living and would indeed be happy to steal their food.

While many stories are told of the Celestial Dog, none are told of Chang Hsien. He just stands there with his bow raised to the skies — a perpetual, fixed image of protection.

The absence of stories often indicates that the idea is of some antiquity and it was with some excitement that I came across mention of the "arrow shooting Chang song contest" in connection with the semi-autonomous kingdom of Mustang. Mustang is Tibetan in culture but is on the South side of that country — that is to say the side furthest from China. The Chang mentioned is an alcoholic drink which, although widely drunk at all times, is the ceremonial drink of that people — In Mandarin Ch'ang 唱 means "to sing" and Ch'ang 鬯 means "sacrifical spirits". The fit is too neat to be coincidental.

Chang is made from barley which is placed in a jar of water with a little yeast. The jar is sealed for three or four weeks. The resulting porridge is then mixed with water and turns into a drink similar to cider. There appear to be two such festivals a year. One from the fifth to seventh day of the third month and the other from fourteenth to sixteenth of the seventh month. The first festival falls on the Chinese grave sweeping ceremony Ch'ing Ming, and the second in the solar period denoting the beginning of autumn, and the harvest. We know from other sources that wine was freely given to the spirits at important festivals in ancient times — our own word spirits indicates a similar relationship of alcohol and the other world. We also know the autumn was a time of feasting; of giving, of receiving in excess of what one had given and of giving even more in return. The arrow shooting Chang song feast succeeded planting and harvesting for the spokesman cried out, "Let there be arrow shooting and song with beer. Do the donkeys stop and rest and make merry, do the animals in the field drink beer? No! I say to you, you are not animals. Each year from the fifth to the seventh day of the third month you must drink and sing and be merry ... Drink, for you are not mules but men; mules do not drink and the

Chang is good. Let the women sing, for that is the wish of the Three Holies."

Chang is also central to a Mustang wedding, marking each step of the way. Chinese and Tibetan sexual mores differ to a great extent but there are sufficient correspondences in the wedding ceremony itself to suggest influences. In Mustang, when a man decides he wants to marry a girl he goes to her window at night and whispers "let me in, let me in". The girl will always call back in a loud voice "Go away. Go away". If she likes him she will at the same time let him in and assume parental consent from the father's inaction. They will then go to bed. The next day the boy's father will take a bottle of Chang along to the girl's father who will make the return trip in like manner the following day if the girl agrees. On the day after, the boy himself drinks with his future father-in-law and everything is settled.

On the day of the wedding the girl sets out on a white horse led by a boy who is not a member of either family and whose parents are still living. Along the route old women gather in groups and hold out bowls of Chang while singing songs of advice. The girl dips her finger in the Chang and flicks it around her three times so that it lands on the earth. (The Chinese ceremony demands that both bride and groom pour out a glass of spirits three times in front of the girl's family's ancestor scroll.) Throughout the journey the girl has an arrow placed behind her neck. When she arrives at the house of her husband-to-be this is removed. When she reaches the threshold a lama throws 3 grains of rice over her and the boy's mother gives her turquoise. Quite how the spread of ideas between China and Tibet — and through that country between India and China — came about is not known. It may not have been a contact between two distinct peoples but a continuing association between two cultures stemming from some original common ancestor for both were originally cave dwellers, both are essentially exclusive and the extent of symbolic similarities is striking. It seems clear that there has been a continuous interaction between them since antiquity.

However, cultural similarities themselves are not evidence of sustained contact. The Dogon Tribe of Mali in West Africa are millet growers who live near cliffs which used to be inhabited. They built their villages on a north-south axis. In death the men are buried with their heads to the north but facing west. They are ancestor worshippers and see time as following cycles of 60 years. Their house fronts are images of faces — as were those of China in the Han Dynasty and before. The tortoise has an important ritual significance as protector of the household when the head of the family is away — Pak Tai is protector of the state. The original ancestors of the Dragon were half snakes. The list of correspondence is impressive yet contact cannot be the cause. With Tibet, proximity alone justifies the belief in extensive interaction and its corollary that Chang Hsien is a personification of the arrow shooting Chang drinking contest as well as of an earlier rite connected with birth.

Lu Pan:
Patron of Builders

In Chinese religion protection is high on the list of divine duties, so it comes as no surprise to find that each calling, guild and association pays specific attention to a patron deity. Even prostitutes have their patron Gods to whom they pray for generous clients. But prostitutes do not belong to a recognized structured organization and so the Gods they worship will vary from city to city and even from brothel to brothel. Among those who follow more acceptable professions there is much greater consistency. Kuan Kung, for example, is the protecting deity of restaurant-keepers and money-changers among other trades. But, whereas Kuan Kung's popularity is general, there are Gods whose sole function is to be patron of a trade. Of these Lu Pan, patron of builders, bricklayers, housepainters and carpenters, is the best known.

In Hong Kong his importance can be seen as a reflection of the building boom that has taken place over the last twenty years but there is another reason why he is accorded respect — he is the guardian spirit of the act of house-building. We can understand this more clearly when we appreciate that a man's first responsibility is not to the state but to his family. The home of his family is thus of the greatest importance. We have seen that the most common type of temple is built on the same plan as a house. The Chinese house is in itself an image of the entire Chinese symbolic system. It has to be if it is to protect its inmates. The building of such a house must not be done without invoking as much good fortune as possible. Not only is great attention paid to the exact site but the Chinese calendar is consulted to select auspicious days on which to start. The single most important event in the building of a house is the placing in position of the main beam, which holds together the external walls and supports the roof. This beam is placed in position on a day dictated by the Chinese calendar as favouring this purpose and not at the state in construction when it is necessary to do so. Thus the main beam may very well be erected before work has started on the foundations. It is then left, supported by wooden tressels while the rest of the building grows up around it. Now that buildings do not require a central beam and are thrown up at great speed little thought is given to auspicious days. Even Lu Pan is not always prayed to as he would have been before.

All the trades involved in house building worship Lu Pan and, if the stories relating his supernatural interventions are to be believed, their trust is not misplaced. Two of these stories concern contractors who faced impending imperial disapproval.

In the first, the contractor who had been instructed to build the Mahakala Miao, the Mongol Temple, designed the roof out of proportion. Realizing this too late he foresaw disaster and contemplated suicide. On the evening prior to putting his decision into effect he went as normal to have dinner at the work site canteen. The regular cook had fallen ill and his replacement overseasoned the dishes. The workers complained but all the substitute could say in defence was "I have put too much salt in." The contractor saw another meaning in the words, "Add another set of eaves." He did so and achieved a successful novelty.

Novelty was a much sought after commodity. Emperors particularly wished to have their stature given permanent expression. The obvious way of doing this was to have built memorable temples or palaces which would ensure that their fame lived on, recognized by future generations. Even the Mongol emperors, who at first were quite prepared to burn all the cities and depopulate the countryside in order to create a vast plain on which to feed their horses, soon became sufficiently sinified to see the value of taxing the people ånd building memorials to their own magnificence. One of the Yuan emperors desired a summer house, insisting on originality. The contractor racked his brains but could not come up with a suitable design. One day an employee of his, aware of the problem, went to a tea house and found himself sitting next to an old man who had with him an empty bird cage of curious design. He knew immediately that this was the answer to his employer's problem. He asked the man to sell it to him but the price asked — 1,000 taels — was far more than he could afford. When the workman went home he found the cage on the table, having been left by a man whose description fitted his recent acquaintance. The next morning he took it to the contractor who was so delighted that he paid the sum immediately. The old man was, of course, Lu Pan.

These interventions on the part of Lu Pan give the impression of a benevolent disinterested character who might have been himself an imperial contractor who had fallen foul of court intrigue, perhaps, and was thus on hand to prevent his colleagues in trade from similar suffering. There is little in what we know of him to sustain this view. We cannot even be sure that he was once a man. If he was a mortal he is one of·the earliest historical characters to be raised to the Heavens, and the stories that are attached to his name are a mixture of myth and legend. Let us first deal with the mythic elements.

Born in 606 BC in the kingdom of Lu, he was a skilled carpenter who became a recluse, giving up his trade to delve into the secrets of magic. He retired to Li Shan mountain to perfect his skills. The people of that area, fearing his powers, murdered him. The deed was followed by a severe drought which convinced the people of their error. They built a shrine to him. In his disembodied state he returned to Li Shan to complete his study of magic before finally ascending to Heaven, where he repaired the pillars of Heaven and built a palace for Hsi Wang Mu, Queen of Western Heaven. On his ascension he left his axe and saw as a legacy.

Another story tells us that while he was still young his father was taken and killed by marauding troops from the neighbouring state. Lu Pan thereupon showed his mastery of carpentry by carving the perfect image of his father. He set it facing the enemy state and for three years drought plagued that place. Only when they returned the body and paid appropriate compensation did he cleave the image in two.

The idea of drought seems to be important and, as we know, drought is connected with imbalance or disharmony in the system. It is no coincidence that he is worshipped on the thirteenth day of the sixth month. This is the month when the rains are expected. If the rains do not come there is disaster. This day is also that of the God of Wine, suggesting that if all is well there are great celebrations. There is no suggestion here that Lu Pan can create water, only that he can arrange its absence. To understand this we must look at the theory of the five elements. All matter is made up from the interaction of earth, water, wood, fire and metal. These elements mutually produce and destroy each other.

Thus the cycle of mutual production is

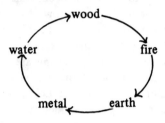

and the cycle of mutual destruction is

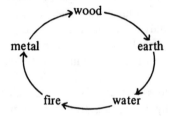

If we look at the second cycle, that of destruction, we can interpret it in the following way. Earth destroys water but the process is controlled by wood (which destroys earth). Lu Pan, carpenter, can control the destruction of water but, as we can see from the first cycle, he can do nothing about its creation.

The idea of disharmony finds further reverberations in the clear implication that the pillars that supported Heaven were in a bad state of repair. He repaired them thus restoring stability. A stable system is one in which there is an harmonious integration of this world and the next. A man must honour his dead father. If, like Lu Pan, he was unable to, something was very wrong. He not only regained possession of his father but he built the palace of Hsi Wang Mu in which live the spirits of the dead. To the extent that the dead live on in the memory of the living they have an honoured place in Heaven. The souls of the dead fly on the back of a crane to Western Heaven. By establishing a residence for them he had secured their position, and thus restored peace to the living.

There is an insistant logic to this story, which like all mythic logic is too complex in its reference to be easily summarized or reformulated.

Even the designated year of birth seems to add an echo of the same ideas 606 BC, two years before Lao Tzu's year of birth, is, in the 60 year cycle, the year Chia Yin whose element is wood. Chia 甲 can be translated as finger nails; Yin 寅 means "take care of". Fingernails and hair are almost universally associated with the vital force of the spirit, for, on death, these two continue to grow, and when the flesh has disappeared they, with the bones and teeth, remain. To take care of the fingernails is to honour to spirit of the dead.

Up till now we have been in the presence of pure myth unfettered by historical facts. There is some doubt as to whether he was a real person. References to him are matter-of-fact and involve other persons whose existence is in no doubt, but there is a problem of dating.

His dates are unknown but he is said to have flourished at about 470 BC. He was an engineer and an inventor of devices. The number of machines and devices whose invention is attributed to him is large and these attributions should not always be accepted. Necessity is the mother of invention and the period in which Lu Pan is supposed to have lived was a time of great social upheaval.

He is credited with inventing the use of a block and tackle to lower heavy coffins into the ground; a rotary grain mill made of two chiselled stones placed one on top of the other to grind hulled rice and wheat to produce flour; a rice huller made of clay and plaited bamboo; the anchor lock which is a thin wooden slat which, slipped into a crack in door handles, keeps the door firmly shut; and the boat hook fender to be used in close combat on water, either to fend off or to pull in the enemy. The list goes on. Doubts have been expressed as to the validity of some of these attributions – especially the grain mill – but as yet no one has been able to date the appearance of these inventions sufficiently accurately to definitively disprove the attributions.

Lu Pan is usually referred to as a "mechanic". Such a person would have been ill-educated in the scholarly subjects and have little or no theoretical appreciation of his own work. Intuition, common sense, rule of thumb and of course, manual skill would have been his means. Lu Pan appears as a jack of all trades willing to turn his talents to any problem that came his way. At the time in which he lived "mechanics" or "artificers" though of low status were beginning to make their presence felt. It seems clear that a technical revolution was occurring at this time despite the opposition of the bureaucrats and scholars who derided the possibility of many of the inventions. Ill-educated, the mechanics found themselves easy butts of the scholars' ridicule.

They could not answer with their tongues only with their hands. However, the practicality of their claims could not be denied for long and a shift in status occurred. Once this happened the pendulum of credibility swung the other way and soon mechanics were being credited with near magical abilities. The story is told of a mechanic, Yen Shih, who built a robot which looked and acted like a human, yet was entirely built from artificial materials. He appeared with his creation before King Mu of Chou and was nearly executed for his pains because his robot began to flirt with the royal concubines. Only by dismantling it could Yen Shih persuade the King it was not human. This story is interesting in that it explicitly states that Yen Shih was not Chinese but lived to the west of China. This suggests that influences were being felt, perhaps, from Persia, possibly even from Greece, as early as 500 BC. The story ends with Yen Shih being brought to China in state.

Lu Pan also, for a time, was favoured by royalty. He was patronized by the Duke of Ch'u — one of the most powerful of the kingdoms. This Duke had acquisitive designs on the neighbouring kingdom of Sung and Lu Pan built a "cloud stepping ladder" — presumably a manoeuvrable turret such as was used in Europe during the middle ages — with which the Duke's army would be able to scale the walls of the enemy capital. On hearing of these plans Mo Ti, a philosopher who preached his belief that universal love should be enforced by laws and coercion, ordered the members of his ascetic, militaristic, religious order to go and help that capital while he himself went alone to Ch'u to argue the Duke out of his intentions. His arguments were succinct and pointed and the Duke would have agreed not to attack if he hadn't been infatuated with his new machines and wanted to try them out. Mo Ti saw that the only solution was to engage Lu Pan in a mock battle. Lu Pan launched nine assaults with his machines but was beaten back each time. Only then did the Duke agree to drop the project.

He may also have dropped Lu Pan at the same time for this is his only recorded intrusion into the world of military engineering.

Let us now turn to the problem of dating. In the myth he is supposed to have been born in 606 BC. Some historians date him as flourishing around 470 BC while Mo Ti did not reach the height of his influence until 50 years later at around 420 BC. The incident quoted above seems to have occurred later still. If this conflict between Lu Pan and Mo Ti was an isolated one we might be able to explain it away. However it is not. Lu Pan is a recurrent figure in the book Mo Tzu and he stands in the same structural relationship with Mo Ti throughout. They are opposed to one another and Lu Pan usually ends up being derided. It is not impossible that he was created as a literary counterpoint to more clearly illustrate Mo Ti's philosophy. In this book he is known as Kungshu P'an(公輸盤). Kungshu is an old surname that has long since disappeared from use.

Mo Ti's philosophy was a puritan one. He disliked luxury, pleasure-seeking and the misuse of power. He preached a hard, stoic creed which he lived out with his followers in Spartan communities. He placed usefulness on a pinnacle and poured scorn on what was not useful. One day he was told of a marvellous feat performed by Lu Pan. The mechanic had invented a "wooden bird" on which he rode high up into the sky where he stayed for three days. Mo Ti said, "Your achievement in constructing this bird is not comparable with that of a carpenter in making a linch pin — any achievement which is beneficial to man may be said to be skilful while anything not beneficial may be said to be clumsy." Curiously the same book contains another version of the story in which Mo Ti spent three years making a kite which was wrecked after one day's trial. When his followers insisted on flattering him he replied, "It is not as clever as making a wooden ox-yoke peg." Another sage, hearing of the story is credited with the reply "Mo Tzu is indeed ingenious but perhaps he knows more about making yoke pegs than wooden kites" — a hit at Mo Ti's utilitarianism. We have here two versions of the story; the first is clearly more effective as propaganda for Mo Ti and it is this one that is most remembered.

Most writers on Chinese life see kite-flying as being purely a game though placing its origins in its use by the military as a means of signalling information. Kite flying is a game and no doubt did have other utilitarian uses but it also had strong symbolic importance. It only occurs at certain times of the year. The ninth day of the ninth month, the festival of Chung Yeung, is a grave-visiting, height-seeking, kite-flying festival. Legend has it that one Huan Ching was warned by a magician to flee with his family to a high mountain. He took the advice and so avoided a great unspecified catastrophe. We have here an equation of height and good fortune, kites, because they go so much higher, give added force to this equation. The spring, grave-sweeping festival of *Ch'ing Ming* is, in the south, the other period in which kite flying is very much in evidence. We noted in the introduction that these two festivals lie virtually on the spring and autumn equinoxes at which times the forces of *Yin* and *Yang* are balanced. Peter Goullart reported a similar custom among the people of Likiang. In July, the critical month before the rainy season young children made balloons from wood and rough paper. They attached a lit bundle of grass below it and the hot air made the balloon swell up and rise into the air. The higher it rose the better the luck. No doubt they used balloons because the winds would not have been strong enough for a kite.

Lu Pan, invoker of harmony and builder of the palace of the Queen of Western Heaven, is very well suited for his position as guardian of house building and of the trades involved in this construction. His symbols in the picture are the set square and plane of a carpenter. More usually he is associated with the axe, which is associated with *Fu,* to begin and has a possible secondary association with, *Fu,* happiness. The axe is symbolic of the marriage go-between and the Chinese proverb "brandishing one's axe at the door of Lu Pan" is the equivalent of "teaching your grandmother to suck eggs".

Lei Kung:
God of Thunder

It may seem strange that, having its origins in nature worship, Chinese religion boasts of few major Gods overseeing the natural forces. There are, in fact, a wealth of such Gods but they are not of the first rank. Of these one of the most important is Lei Kung, Lord of Thunder.

Thunder, accompanied by lightning, is one of the most awesome forces of nature. In the West it was felt to be the voice and instrument of God, and still is if only jokingly. In Buddhist thought, too, thunder and lightning are seen as the force and power by which evil is punished. These functions do not seem to have been originally ascribed to thunder in China where it was seen as a benign force producing rain. Nevertheless some of these other concepts have, through Buddhist influence, attached themselves to this deity.

Lei Kung was personified at about the beginning of the Christian era and was then depicted as a strong handsome man who held a hammer and chisel and whose movements were punctuated by the rumbling of strings of drums. His image was transformed about a thousand years ago into a bird-like creature with a face like a monkey's. It is believed that this new form derives from the Garuda, a mythical bird-like creature with teeth who was messenger for the Hindu God, Vishnu.

Sometimes considered to be Chief Minister of the Ministry of Thunder and Storms, Lei Kung presides over the deities responsible for lightning, wind and rain. He assists in providing rain for harvests and, when worshipped, he is usually accompanied by Yu Shih, the Master of Rain.

As with all natural phenomena which occur at unseasonable times, portents are ascribed to it. When there is thunder and lightning this means that political change is in the air.

Lei Kung is the God of Thunder and it is he who hurls thunderbolts to the earth. The Goddess of Lightning, Tien Mu, merely flashed her mirror on the intended victim to ensure his aim. It is she who produces the light but the otherwise invisible thunderbolt which causes the damage.

Anyone who has lived with the Chinese knows that noise has great social value. A silent game of mahjong would not have many takers. Noise means involvement in the group. We saw that when society was reconstituted in its ideal form at times of eclipses there was great noise and banging of drums. Noise has positive social value because it is the overt sign of togetherness and thus that all is well. The noise of thunder — caused by the beating of drums — is believed to scare off evil spirits.

When Buddhism spread throughout China the idea of thunder and lightning as forces of punishment gradually became incorporated. These ideas were in any case natural extensions of earlier beliefs and may indeed have existed prior to Buddhist influences without being stressed. Lightning was seen by the Buddhists as the divine force that shatters false belief. That this aspect is treated humourously in a number of stories suggests that it is paid lip service to. Thus we are told that on one occasion Lei Kung wished to punish an old woman who was beating her daughter-in-law but that he was prevented from doing so when she threw a cloth over his head. He was helpless until the rain washed it away. Even when he was not unsighted his aim seems not to have been the best, despite the light from Tien Mu's mirror, for there are several other stories that attest to his striking down the wrong person. When he did so, however, he always admitted his mistake and dropped a bottle of some divine unguent which, when applied, effected an immediate cure. He was clumsy in other matters too for one day he got caught in the branches of a tree and had to request assistance from a mortal to regain his freedom. He rewarded his liberator with a book which contained the secrets of summoning thunder and rain, curing sickness and assuaging sorrow. On giving it, he warned the man only to call him when there was pressing need as he, Lei Kung, had a bad character and easily lost his temper. All this is a far cry from the high seriousness with which the Gods are usually accorded.

There are however, two categories of people who are most predisposed to being struck by lightning. The first is anyone who spills rice on the floor or who treads it into the ground, the other is the unburied dead. If there is a coffin in the house when a thunderstorm threatens, it is covered with grass to make it look like a haystack. As rice symbolizes life there seems to be a connection of ideas. One explanation may be that the unburied dead are an anomalous category. They are dead but still in the world of the living. Treading rice into the ground is a symbolic statement of the obverse, but equally anomalous, state of affairs, the living being placed in the earth. Anomalous categories are dangerous for they are not consistent with balance and harmony. The God of Thunder must therefore show his disapproval.

Chung K'uei:
The Exorcist

If the afterlife is a massive bureaucracy with departments overseeing every conceivable facet of existence, then everything that happens is capable of being explained. If illness, its cause, its duration and its result have already been inventoried for each occurrence, it would be easy to assume that the Chinese have a fatalistic view of life — such as is often attributed to Moslems. The Chinese, however, have no real sense of an independent inscrutable Heaven which vents its will on the world. If illness visits a man and that man wants a reason, he may fall back on the Buddhist idea that this is the result of bad actions either on the part of himself or of one of his ancestors. The length of one's life depends on virtue and here virtue is implicitly seen as being an attribute of the clan as well as of the person. There is also a strong belief that the Gods gamble with people's fates. When the Gods of the Northern and Southern measures are found playing chess in the woods they are playing with people's fates. As this story goes on to prove, the Gods are capable of being influenced by judicious bribes. "If you grant me this, I shall make an offering of a suckling pig" is the kind of silent — or not so silent — invocation that may be made in a temple when requesting divine intercession. The Chinese are not fatalists.

While illness may result from lack of virtue or the random throw of some deity's dice, it is more commonly assumed to be caused by the presence of an evil spirt. Here we have a recognition of something akin to a random malevolence, a being who is not controlled by the dictates of Heaven. Evil spirits may be ghosts of the dead who remain in the vicinity of the grave but more usually no explanation is made of their origins because far more important is the desire to escape their influence.

We have already seen some of the defence system: the *bath kua,* — or eight trigrams — the mirror, the door Gods, the image of Kuan

Kung who faces the entrance and the sprig of peach blossom placed on the lintel over the doorway. But this is by no means the full range of devices. We have here another – the image of Chung K'uei, the exorcist.

The story has come down to us that Chung K'uei was a physician from Shensi Province. Physicians were usually scholars who had failed in the public examinations and had no other trade, apart from teaching, to fall back on. Having presumably already taken this exam once, perhaps twice, before, Chung K'uei again presented himself and again failed. Believing that he had been unfairly deprived of his rightful honours by corrupt examiners, a situation not without precedent, he committed suicide on the steps of the Imperial Palace. The emperor, Ming Huang (712–756 AD) was kept ignorant of the fact but the act of suicide had desecrated the precincts of the Palace so allowing malign spirits to enter. Not long after, the emperor succumbed to a fever in which he dreamt that he was being persecuted by a red demon called "Emptiness and Devastation". The ghost of Chung K'uei appeared and exorcized the evil spirit. The emperor was immediately cured. Chung K'uei then informed the emperor of all that had happened. His body was exhumed and reburied with full rights in the green robe of the Imperial clan. His portrait was painted and he was given the title "Great Spiritual Chaser of Demons for the Whole Empire."

What are we to make of this story? The best interpretation seems to be that we are involved with the personification of a plant. There is a kind of mallow named Chung K'uei (終葵), identical in tone, which has the magical property of warding off demons. The leaves of this plant are used as poultices and have the medical property of relaxing patients who are feverish. The mallow is purplish in colour and this may be suggested the imperial connection. Personified, he assumed the surname Chung (鍾), which incorporates the idea of gold, earth and centre, and K'uei (馗) which contains the idea "in charge of weakness." His image was placed above the door during the fifth – the most dangerous – month. This is the month which lies in the central hall of summer when *Yang* is at its zenith. It seems odd that summer should be the season of bad luck. Perhaps it is because this is the time of the first harvest. This is the time when most care must be taken. The Gods of mountains and rivers, the ancestors and the dragons of the seas are all appeased at this time. Red is the colour of this season and the red demon was called "Emptiness and Devastation". If the weather is bad or malign forces ruin the harvest the effect is more disastrous than if these forces descended at other times of the year.

We see him here in his usual stance, engaged in ferocious combat. His weapons are a sword and fan on which there is a magical inscription for warding off spirits. Translated, the inscription reads "Lead on happiness, restore the hall". His face too is a weapon — so awesome is it that it alone is capable of scaring any spirit who might dare to oppose him. From his hat dangle symbolic peaches — for immortality — and around his head a bat is circling. The bat is not, as it at first seems, the object of Chung K'uei's attack but represents happiness — the association is linguistic.

Chung K'uei is the most popular, but not the Chief Minister in Heaven's Ministry of Exorcisms. The Chief Minister is Chang Tao-ling, first "pope" of the Taoist "church". It is his image that we see riding a tiger and wielding a sword below the *baht kua*. We have already traced his historical career in the introduction. He and his descendants have taken the title T'ien Shih or Master of Heaven and, until the Communist takeover, inhabited a palace in the Dragon Tiger mountain in Kiangsi Province. In the cellars of this palace it was believed there were jars in which exorcised spirits had been imprisoned. He too is connected with the fifth day of the fifth month as we see from the following legend. With his sword he vanquished the "Five Poisonous Animals". These are the scorpion, centipede, snake, toad and spider. He placed them in the box in which he had distilled the Elixir of Life. On the fifth day of the fifth month they yielded their venom which contributed to the final and pure Elixir which he swallowed at the age of one hundred and twenty three years old, upon doing which he left the mortal coil and ascended to the Heavens. These five poisonous animals are worshipped in image by those who seek protection for an only son. A tincture of the Five Poisons is used as a remedy for rheumatism and coughs among other afflictions.

Exorcism is a Taoist speciality. If a building is haunted or if there is an epidemic, a priest will be called in to expel the malign influences. The fan, the scroll, a sword made of peach wood or pieces of cash bound together are his necessary instruments as he prepares for combat. The priest will use other devices likely to attain his end. He may spray water from his mouth or smear the blood of a cock around the doorposts. He will chant various formulae and place talismans at various points then, working along a circular path, he will herd the spirits off the premises.

On the seventh day of the seventh month is the festival of the Hungry Ghosts when the spirits of the dead descend to share in the bounty of the harvest. These ghosts are shepherded to and from this visit by Chang, astride his tiger and wielding his sword.

We have traced Chang's historical career but this has been supplemented by mythic additions. According to this he was born in 35 AD. This date was probably reached by subtracting the length of life attributed to him from his date of death which is not exactly known but was probably about 157 AD. Born in Chekiang Province he moved to the West where he studied alchemy and cultivated mental abstraction — meditation was practiced long before Buddhism arrived in China. In the course of these pursuits he was presented with a mystic treatise by Lao Tzu himself and with the help of this book he produced the elixir of life.

Another time he was told where to find the writings of the Three Emperors of Antiquity. He followed their prescriptions and obtained the power of flying, of leaving his body and other similar abilities. With the further aid of a Goddess he became capable of walking among the stars of dividing mountains and seas, of commanding the wind and thunder and of defeating multitudes of demons.

The interesting thing about this story is that it considers Chang to have been an alchemist and wholly ignores his health cult. Chang's descendants followed one another as Masters of Heaven, a title decreed to them by the emperor in 424 AD. They made their money from selling talismans and diplomas. However, their influence was that of ecclesiastical jurisdiction over a school of thought — one among many — and not absolute heads of an organization. Their importance reached a peak during the Sung Dynasty and it was at this time that they were granted the domain of Dragon Tiger Mountain. They remained in favour during the Yuan and Ming Dynasties but fell finally in the Ch'ing Dynasty when they were demoted to a fairly low rank.

The story of the competing Taoist schools over the last 1800 years is an interesting if complex story — but we must now return to Chung K'uei for his story is only half told. Not only is he a divine exorcist but, under the name K'uei Hsing, he is the Star God of Literature. In this guise the story goes that Chung K'uei was a brilliant scholar who passed out first in the metropolitan examinations and should thus have been presented with a rose of gold. However, Chung was so ugly and deformed that the emperor refused him the gift. Miserable and rejected Chung threw himself into the sea where he was saved from drowning by a sea monster on whose back he ascended to Heaven. He was given the position of overseeing scholars and ensuring that they received their dues.

That Chung K'uei the exorcist, should have seemed appropriate as God of Literature is not, at first sight, understandable. The reason for this may lie in the fact that literature was the prime subject of the imperial exams which had to be passed before one could gain entrance to the bureaucracy. Ability in literature is the pre-requisite for ability in Government. Good government ensures a peaceful nation. Government officials acting to the best of their ability produce social harmony, thus exorcizing the malign forces that reign at times of imbalance in the system. This may be the answer or it may be that the connection stems from the feudal period when the learned were experts in such fields as cosmology, ritual magic and other such fields. A more direct association of ideas may also have played its part in relating literature and exorcism. Chung K'uei is wide-eyed. He is thus able to know the true nature of his opponent. Literature was the highest branch of knowledge, necessitating great analytic skills. If anyone was capable of knowing the true nature of things it was the Literati.

Wong Tai Sin:
The Great Immortal Wong

This God after whom a district in Kowloon has been named has had a meteoric success in the Colony. The God arrived in Hong Kong in 1915, brought by a man and his son who came from Kwangtung carrying a painting of him. They installed the painting and an altar in a small temple in Wanchai, Hong Kong and it appears that his efficacy soon became public knowledge. Six years later an organization was established to collect funds to build the God his own temple. The funds came in and a site was found. Backed by Lion Rock and facing the sea, its geomantic position was excellent. The temple was built in 1921. On this site too were built many other altars and temples to other Gods such as Buddha, and Confucius. In 1956 the temples and gardens were opened to the public for a nominal fee of ten cents and its popularity can be estimated from the fact that it had, up to 1977, raised $4 million for educational purposes and another $4 million to rebuild the temple in 1973. Not all this money will have been raised by the ten cent fee, contributions for special prayers are extremely common.

The efficacy of Wong Tai Sin is such that almost everybody I have met has some story. I am told that he is prayed to for racing tips and that he cured a man who had been languishing in hospital for three months and whose ailment had been undiagnosed by western specialists. Another man always went to pray at this temple on the New Year. One year he decided not to bother. The subsequent ill luck that dogged him ensured that he did not omit his duties again.

Who, then, is Wong Tai Sin? The legend tells of a shepherd boy who lived in a remote part of Chekiang Province. One day at the age of 15 he was blessed by an immortal who taught him the art of making the elixir of life by refining cinnabar. He spent the next 40 years on Red Pine Hill living the life of a hermit in a cave. At the end of this period his brother finally tracked him down and — a nice touch —

asked him what had happened to the sheep. Wong Tai Sin took him to a flat area covered with white boulders and transformed them into sheep. It appears he is also called the Red Pine Fairy.

To take a story like this at face value is nonsense. We are told the age at which he is blessed but not the century in which he lived. Again we must look for some other level of meaning.

There is something very familiar about the crucial point of the story — the creation of life from the earth. It was Fu-hsi who introduced husbandry, it was Huang-ti who turned man to an agricultural existence. Both are founder creators of Chinese civilization. The attributes of one relate to the other. If we translate Wong Tai Sin into Mandarin we get Huang Tai Hsien. Huang is, of course, a common surname but it is tempting to posit that Hong Kong's newest God is one of China's oldest. Is there any support for such a theory?

Wong lived in a cave, so did Huang-ti. He is called the Red Pine Fairy (or Immortal) — red is the colour of summer over which season Huang-ti presides; the pine is an emblem of longevity and is used metaphorically for friends who remain true when times are bad. The sheep of the story may very well be goats, called hill-sheep in Chinese. The goat is one of the animals used for sacrifice and is the emblem of the eighth month and year, and symbolizes the end of summer. Using the magic square we see that he was blessed when the first hall of spring (1) had come upon the earth (5) and that he stayed in a cave until the first hall of summer (4) at which time his brother came to look at the state of the flock. He brought the goats to life.

If one is looking for proof it is difficult to see what weight of evidence would meet the necessary requirements. Proof is not something one can hope to attain. All one can do is establish a reasonable possibility. It may seem far-fetched to constantly relate numbers to a magical square and yet, if by doing so one consistently obtains interesting results, one must assume that there is something to be said for the method. I am myself convinced that there is, in China, nothing so new as the very old. One does not go to "a remote part of Chekiang Province" to discover the new, rather the opposite. New Gods may arise and fall in the towns and cities but the old Gods remain in the undisturbed corners of remote districts.

How are the mighty fallen? Huang-ti, the Yellow Emperor — God of the Earth in which the dead are buried; God of the soil which is nourished by the spring waters which contain the spirits of the dead. How great was his efficacy! Guardian of the ancient civilization, creator of marriage and morality, language and lineage. Now worshipped as "Great Immortal Wong".